PROTECTORS OF THE PLANET

ENVIRONMENTAL TRAILBLAZERS FROM 7 TO 97

JAMIE BASTEDO

Red Deer Press

For Brenda
and the many trails we have blazed together

Library and Archives Canada Cataloguing in Publication
Title: Protectors of the planet : environmental trailblazers from 7 to 97 / Jamie Bastedo.
Names: Bastedo, Jamie, 1955- author.
Description: Includes index.
Identifiers: Canadiana 20200181777 | ISBN 9780889955691 (softcover)
Subjects: LCSH: Environmentalists—Biography—Juvenile literature. | LCSH: Environmentalism—Juvenile
literature. | LCSH: Environmental protection—Citizen participation—Juvenile literature. |
LCGFT: Biographies.
Classification: LCC GE55 .B37 2020 | DDC j363.70092—dc23

Publisher Cataloging-in-Publication Data (U.S.)
Names: Bastedo, Jamie, 1955-, author.
Title: Protectors of the Planet : Environmental Trailblazers from 7 to 97 / Jamie Bastedo.
Description: Markham, Ontario : Red Deer Press, 2020. | Summary: "This book introduces 11
inspirational environmental trailblazers carving bold new paths into a better world. They are
heroes dedicated to a noble cause. They are role models empowering us to follow. They are
ordinary people doing extraordinary things to protect the planet" – Provided by publisher.
Identifiers: ISBN 978-0-88995-569-1 (paperback)
Subjects: LCSH Environmentalists—Biography – Juvenile literature. | Conservationists –
Biography – Juvenile literature. | JUVENILE NONFICTION / Science & Nature /
Environmental Conservation & Protection.
Classification: LCC GE55.B378 |DDC 333.720922 – dc23

 Canada Council Conseil des arts
for the Arts du Canada

 ONTARIO ARTS COUNCIL
CONSEIL DES ARTS DE L'ONTARIO
an Ontario government agency
un organisme du gouvernement de l'Ontario

Red Deer Press acknowledges with thanks the Canada Council for the Arts and the Ontario Arts Council for their support of our publishing program. We acknowledge the financial support of the Government of Canada through the Canada Book Fund (CBF) for our publishing activities.

2 4 6 8 10 9 7 5 3 1

Edited for the Press by Peter Carver
Text and cover design by Kong Njo
Printed in Canada by Friesens

www.reddeerpress.com

Never doubt that a small group of thoughtful committed citizens can change the world. Indeed it's the only thing that ever has.

– Margaret Mead, anthropologist

A change is brought about because ordinary people do extraordinary things.

– President Barack Obama

Contents

MAGNIFICENCE MATTERS

··

Kicking Over Logs

If you had spied me back then, prowling alone through the sugar maple forest behind my house, in Kitchener, Ontario, you would have wondered what the heck I was doing. I was that kid kicking over logs, then falling to my knees to seize some wriggling thing in my eager hands. To my seven-year-old brain, this was an alien creature, some rare throwback to dinosaur days, an exotic being that only I knew about. When I later learned that this creature could grow new limbs and tails that were sliced off in death-defying fights, I became even more convinced it came from outer space.

The Red-backed Salamander.

I captured them by the handful, built terrariums for them, and fed them cottage cheese. I tried, unsuccessfully, to raise families of them and show them to my not-so-impressed friends.

Fast-forward and I'm the teenager, ripping out surveyor stakes, one by one, and flinging them out of sight. They marked the footprint of a monster housing project that would flatten a forest close to my heart. It was there that I spotted my first Wood Duck, the most gorgeous duck in North America, with its impossibly painted Darth Vader helmet.

Sail ahead a few years and I'm the rookie graduate student following wolf and caribou tracks through the Yukon wilds, trying hard not to fall off a mountain while stunned by the beauty of it all.

Decades later, I'm a biologist, zooming low over the Arctic tundra, gazing out the bubble window of a chopper as I search for a satellite-collared grizzly bear.

Then, not long ago, there I am, leading tourists from faraway places like Berlin or Bar Harbour, down a lakeside trail near my Yellowknife home. Together we stroke the ancient rock, listen for Yellow-billed Loons, and whistle at the Northern Lights. We sink our souls into some of the biggest, wildest country on Earth.

I sometimes wonder if I would have become a biologist were it not for those Red-backed Salamanders with their mysterious, googly eyes. Ever since those early days, kicking over logs, I've followed a treasure map into a world of wonders, learning all I can about nature, sharing it with others, and doing my best to protect it.

I see my job as guiding people into that world, using every tool I can get my hands on—a winding forest trail, radio broadcasts to tickle your imagination, songs to swap around a campfire, skits to laugh along with, or books to curl up and get lost in—like this one.

> "*I* care to live only to entice people to look at Nature's loveliness."
> – John Muir, *Son of the Wilderness*

People ask me a lot of questions along the way. Who made these tracks? What good are mosquitoes? What if a bear charges? Will I die if I eat this mushroom? We naturalists love questions. But these days, as sinister environmental threats about the future keep bursting into the news, more and more l hear this one: *What can I do?*

My short answer?

Keep hope alive and you'll know what to do. Without hope, we might as well give up right now.

My long answer?

This book.

Where do I find hope for the future? Not kicking over logs looking for cool critters, though I still delight in that. I find hope in the lives of people doing amazing things for the planet.

You are about to meet some pretty awesome people.

A teen activist who risked gunfire to save a forest. A park warden who hiked thousands of miles in the path of the grizzly to help protect wildlife. A young woman who fought impossible odds to pioneer giraffe research in Africa. A teenage girl who barely escaped Nazi Germany and devoted the rest of her days to greening cities. A young climate crusader who lobbies nose-to-nose with the most powerful politicians in the land. And lots more!

Think of the following true-life stories as a human library of people who are painfully aware of the environmental threats to our planet—maybe even our very *civilization*—yet are taking action to fight those threats in positive, sometimes epic, and often fun ways. They are all, as the saying goes, *thinking globally, acting locally,* to help make the world a better place.

The funny thing is, these people are just like you and me. You will see yourself in their stories. Aren't we all looking for a little more meaning and purpose and adventure in our lives? These people have discovered all that in the causes they chose to throw themselves into. And you can too, inspired by their example, fuelled by their hope.

You ask, *What can I do?*

You'll know what to do.

But first, the bad news.

Bad News

It all makes me want to plug my ears. Cover my eyes. Shut my mouth.

Just like those three Japanese monkeys, I don't want to hear it, see it, talk about it.

I'm learning new words and ideas I don't want to know: *biocide, ecocide, ecocatastrophe, disaster fatigue, global dimming, the Sixth Great Extinction.*

I'm hearing record-breaking news I don't want to believe: The deadliest heatwaves. The hottest temperatures. The stormiest weather. The biggest forest fires. The most devastating floods. The highest extinction rates.

Do I even care that these records are now broken year after year?

What am I supposed to do with *that*?

Maybe I have disaster fatigue.

Even as I worked on this book, two earth-shaking studies came out, suggesting that, unless we humans get our eco-act together, an eco-apocalypse is just around the corner. In

October 2018, the Intergovernmental Panel on Climate Change warned that we have only a dozen years to put the brakes on global warming or else we're basically cooked. Then in May of 2019, the United Nations released a massive report on global biodiversity that predicts that we can kiss goodbye a million species within the next few decades.

Then I learned that these twin threats to the biosphere— speciescide (I didn't make that up) and climate change—are intimately connected. If we keep dropping forests and all the species that make them tick, we sap the planet's ability to hold carbon and it gets hotter. When things heat up, more forests burn and species disappear. You get how this works.

Should I stop there?

It gets better. Honest.

But first, let me tell you about a troubling conversation I had with a guy named Ian McAllister, a world-class nature photographer, filmmaker, and author who is featured in this book. He told me things I didn't want to write about.

I asked Ian what keeps him awake at night when he thinks about his children's future.

"I feel sometimes that we're witnessing the tail end of the Earth's magnificence," he told me, "and it's just heartbreaking to think that my kids and their kids might not get to experience its true beauty, that they're entering a very fragile, uncertain time on this planet."

"So, what would it take to turn things around?" I asked Ian.

"We've had so many major wake-up calls in the last few years, it's hard to believe we need any more. From catastrophic weather predicted by the best climate science, to the astonishing statistics around species extinction, you have to ask, 'What extra information do we possibly need to rethink how we live on this planet?' I can't imagine what that would be. We already know more than enough. Now it's just a matter of waking up and taking action."

In the pages that follow, you'll meet Sheila Watt-Cloutier, an Inuit leader from northern Québec. For Sheila and her Arctic world, the climate catastrophe is not decades away. It's real and it's now. The disaster has *already* begun. "We're not preparing for it," she told me. "We're living through it, and it's getting worse." Sheila talks about her Arctic home as the "early warning system" for the state of our planet's climate. She calls her fellow Inuit—and Indigenous people around the world—the "global sentinels of climate change," since they live so closely with the land.

Everyone you'll meet in this book is deeply worried about the current state of our planet, and the hair-raising predictions about its future.

But the good news is: it's not all bad news.

Everyone you'll meet here is also full of hope for the future. Otherwise, why in the world would they spend so much of their lives taking action to protect the planet?

Blazing Trails

I call them environmental trailblazers.

They are pioneers, carving new paths into the wild and unmapped terrain we call the future. They are heroic adventurers dedicated to a noble cause. They are role models and mentors, showing us where we can go when we really care about something. They are outliers, standing apart from regular mortals like you and me, but inviting us to join them. They are young and they are old. They are ordinary people doing extraordinary things to safeguard life on Earth and preserve its magnificence.

This book shines an up-close-and-personal spotlight on the lives of some of Canada's best and brightest environmental leaders. But more than showcasing their exciting work and achievements, I explore the "making of" these trailblazers with a detective's curiosity.

How did they get this way? What factors shaped them as they grew up? Where did their passion for the planet come from?

Was it in their blood? In their brains? Was it where they lived? Their parents? Their teachers? Their friends? Maybe a pivotal book? Was it some random person they bumped into? Some lucky opportunity? A nothing conversation in the schoolyard? How about their past lives? (Just kidding, but who knows?)

These were fun themes to unpack with everyone I interviewed, whether a world-famous giraffe biologist in her mid-80s, or a twelve-year-old girl fighting for her future under the darkening cloud of climate change.

The colorful cast of real-life characters you'll meet in this book covers a fascinating spectrum of environmental *topics*— from wolves to whales—and *places*—from the frozen Arctic tundra to the searing savannah of Africa. Ranging in age from 7 to 97, they include global experts in their field as well as unsung local heroes, any of whom might just light up your inborn affection for nature and rouse you to protect it.

When I interviewed these changemakers, I made a special point to ask each of them what hands-on advice they had for young people like you who want to make a difference. At the end of each chapter, I've distilled their answers into "Trailblazer Tips" to help you carve your own path.

For those of you who want to explore their lives more deeply, or the issues they are tackling, I've also included a "Digging Deeper" section at the back of the book, listing some key references, videos, and websites that helped me tell their story.

In following the trails blazed by these remarkable people, may you discover excellent adventure, deep inspiration, practical advice, and rekindled hope for the future—as I have.

Enjoy the journey!

Trailblazer
|ˈtrāl,blāzər|
Noun

A person who makes a new track through wild country.
One who marks a tree in the forest to point the way.

ENVIRONMENTAL TRAILBLAZERS

"For the first time in eleven years in politics, young people have approached my office to talk with me. Children come and say, 'You have to help us.' I will make sure that Sophia's voice is heard at Queen's Park."

– France Gélinas, Member of Provincial Parliament

SOPHIA MATHUR

Climate Change Champion
Taking to the streets to fight for the future

Home: Sudbury, Ontario
Pursuits: Youth climate activist, dancer, and cat lover

I'm feeling lucky as I dial Sophia Mathur's phone number. It's taken forever to set up this call and, as it turns out, the timing couldn't be better. Since my first email to her months ago, so many amazing things have happened in the youth climate movement, in her hometown of Sudbury, across Canada, and around the world. I know, too, that it's been a challenging time for Sophia and her family, dealing with the craziest winter in Sudbury's history, plus the slipping away of her beloved grandfather.

I learned that, whatever's going on in Sophia's world, it's usually tough to track down a super busy activist like her. I managed to jump through a narrow window in her packed calendar between yet another trip to Ottawa to lobby the

Canadian Parliament—she's been doing that since she was six—and a trip to Washington to lobby the United States Congress.

When Sophia picks up, I discover I'm in for a fun conference call, with her mother and fellow climate warrior, Cathy, on one side and, on the other, her sometimes annoying cat, Grizabella.

BORN INTO ACTIVISM

"We are certain of the following: emissions resulting from human activities are substantially increasing the atmospheric concentrations of greenhouse gases, resulting in an additional warming of the Earth's surface. These long-lived gases require immediate reductions in emissions from human activities to stabilize their concentrations at today's levels . . . "

Prophetic, troubling words from the first Intergovernmental Panel on Climate Change, well known to climate activists like Sophia as the IPCC.

The "today" they were talking about was way back in 1990, many years before Sophia was born. The panel, launched by the United Nations and made up of scientists from around the world, predicted that by the year 2050, when Sophia turns 43, atmospheric carbon dioxide will double, global temperatures will skyrocket by up to 4.5°C, and seas could rise by half a meter. "If this occurs," the panel concluded, "consequent changes may have a significant impact on society."

Among the first IPCC scientists to ring the climate alarm bell was an Indian biochemist named Dr. Sukhdev Mathur, Sophia's grandfather.

She calls him Daddu.

Sophia's mother, Cathy, is also no stranger to climate change activism. After teaching high school chemistry and biology in Sudbury for many years, she quit her job in 2004 in response to her gnawing dread over the impacts of climate change on the world's children, including her own. Environmental activism eventually became the new focus of her work, through the Citizens' Climate Lobby, or CCL, a fast-growing grassroots organization that lobbies governments to clean up their climate act.

Cathy's fears about climate change rose to a flashpoint in 2007 with the release of the fourth IPCC report. Its messages were basically the same as the first report that Sophia's grandfather helped write.

The Earth is warming.

Time is running out.

Do something!

But the language was punchier, the evidence now indisputable. And this report introduced new and scary threats like: "abrupt or irreversible changes," "multiple extreme weather events," and "tipping points" beyond which there's no turning back. On top of all this, it concluded that these sweeping changes—to the air, land, oceans, and ice—were happening *way* faster than ever predicted by Sophia's grandfather.

When she heard this news on the radio, Cathy's knees gave out from under her. "I practically collapsed into my chair," she wrote on the CCL website. "I was very healthy, forty years old, and pregnant with my third daughter. What would life be like for my daughter when *she* was forty years old? Time stood still. Seconds later, I grabbed my very pregnant belly.

I promised that little girl inside of me that Mommy would do whatever she could to make sure her world would be okay forty years from now."

➤ Cathy promised baby Sophia she would do all she could to make the world a safer place to grow up.

A year after that little girl was born, her mother attended a Climate Bootcamp in Montreal, run by former U.S. Vice President and climate crusader, Al Gore. "I thanked him for helping me keep the promise to my baby. He looked at me and said, 'Can I have a hug?' I said, 'Yes!' What an honor. What a great hug!"

By the time she was six, Sophia was already full of questions about her mother's work. Like, "What's the difference between *lobbying* and *protesting*?" After hashing it out with her mother, here's what little Sophia came up with: "Lobbying is like protesting except you're nice and there's no police in the room."

At age seven, in September 2014, Sophia and her family put on their best runners and marched through the streets of New York City with over 300,000 other activists in the

Sophia has been marching, lobbying, and fund-raising for positive climate action since she was a little girl.

People's Climate March, which was the largest climate change event the world had ever seen.

Two years later, at age nine, she was giving out hand-drawn art cards to members of the U.S. Congress in Washington, with cat-friendly messages like, *Don't Cheetah the Climate*, and *A carbon tax is a purr-fect solution*. Turns out that Sophia was the first kid to *ever* lobby Congress. She was a guinea pig to see how they would react—and they loved her. They listened. She paved the way for other kids to follow her through that heavily guarded gateway to power.

When Sophia was ten, she and her parents hopped in their electric car and drove to Toronto to see her mom's climate change hero, Vice President Al Gore, at a special screening of his latest movie, *An Inconvenient Sequel*. Sophia got to shake his hand, give him one of her homemade art cards, and pose with him for a picture. Among the VIPS gathered in the theater was Canada's Minister of Environment and Climate Change, Catherine McKenna, who Sophia tracked down for an autograph, a friendly chat, and a pinky promise to make the world safer for children. After Sophia captured the moment on Twitter, the Minister Tweeted right back, saying, "Kids get it! Pinky promise to work together to tackle climate change and get moms, dads, and grandparents to do their part too!"

➤ Sophia and her parents meet former U.S. Vice President and global climate change crusader, Al Gore, at a screening of his latest film in Toronto.

> *Former federal Minister of Environment and Climate Change, Catherine McKenna, makes a pinky promise with Sophia to make the world safer for children.*

Back in Sudbury, Sophia stuck to her pinky promise by launching a city-wide campaign to fight plastic pollution. She started by lobbying restaurants and bars to stop automatically handing out plastic drinking straws. Turns out there wasn't a lot of debate. Most businesses just said: "Yes, we'll do it!" One restaurant manager reported a ninety percent reduction in straw use after talking with Sophia. She and her friends then swung their sights to Sudbury's City Hall, convincing councilors to rethink their waste collection program and cut way back on plastics chucked in the landfill.

Meanwhile, Minister McKenna knuckled down on getting a federal carbon tax in place across the country, a goal that Sophia and her mother's lobby group had been pushing politicians to do for years.

All this environmental muscle work in just the first decade of Sophia's life! It's no lie to say she has been living and breathing environmental activism since before she was born.

> **"C**atherine McKenna, our Environment Minister,
> is a person I really look up to because she's just amazing.
> She really inspires me and makes me think that I would
> like a job like hers one day.**"**

CLIMATE CHANGE HUG

"You two are quite a team," I say, after finally connecting with Sophia and her mom.

"I'm just here to fill in any details you might need, Sophia," Cathy says.

"That's okay, Mom, I guess."

"So, you give me a nudge if you want me to add anything. And let me know if I get a little annoying."

"Mom, stop. Just stop."

"You know, Jamie," Cathy says, "she's a pre-teen and might get a little annoyed."

"Mom, *sto-op*!"

"And Sophia," I say, "if *I* get annoying, you let me know, too, okay?"

I hear mother-daughter laughter.

"Now, Sophia, I know your mom is kind of within ear-shot, but would you say that she's been one of your role models?"

"She is my mentor. She helps me stay safe on social media. She teaches me a lot, and I love her."

"Aaah," Cathy sighs.

"Happy Mother's Day!" Sophia says.

"Do you ever feel like you're climbing on your mom's bandwagon?"

"At first, the fact that my mom cared so much, how she wanted to do all this for us children—that meant the world to me. Now I realize that the climate crisis really *is* an important issue, no matter what my mom thinks."

"Do you think growing up in Sudbury shaped who you are and what you do?"

"This town is generally very big on the environment because we used to be a moonscape before we started the whole re-greening thing. That really affected how I started caring for the environment and thinking about the future."

"I remember hitchhiking through Sudbury in the seventies," I say. "I'd heard about the town's nasty history of pollution from nickel mining and how that wrecked the land around it. But it was amazing to see it with my own eyes. Moonscape is right! In fact, NASA's moon vehicle had just left. Have you and your classmates been part of that re-greening process, or was it looking pretty good by the time you were born?"

"As long as I can remember, Sudbury has been a beautiful green city. But I heard that back then it was pretty ugly. We've had a few school presentations about it. It's such a success story."

"Do you get out in those green woods?"

"I live near a forest, so I do get a lot of time to play outdoors. I'm also a big fan of dancing, music, math, and reading."

"You did say *math*?"

"Yes, I love math. I was born as a *Math*-ur, right?"

"I get it! What do you like to read?"

"I like to read about cats. I'm a big fan of fiction. Sometimes I read non-fiction to learn new things."

"About climate change, for instance?"

"For sure. But I prefer the words, climate *breakdown*."

"Why is that difference important?"

"Because the term 'climate change' isn't scary. It's not accurate. It doesn't get people's attention. The climate *is* changing, but we're going into much more than that now."

"You want to scare people?"

"Not really scare them, but get them to see there's something more going on than just *change*. It's more urgent. It's not something I can just go out and fix tomorrow. When adults hear the words 'climate breakdown' from a kid, they tend to listen better, to think more."

"Why is that?"

"Because today's kids are going to be *way* more impacted than today's adults. I lobby politicians to stop saying the words, 'climate change' and say 'climate breakdown' or 'climate crisis' instead. Some are actually making the switch."

"What about the rest of your family? Are they as gung-ho as you and your mom?"

"My dad is a doctor and lobbies for environmental improvements in the health system. There's this thing called the Lancet Countdown (lancetcountdown.org) that raises awareness of the serious impacts of climate change on everybody's health. He and I are working on that. But my mom generally does a lot more. My dad sort of keeps us grounded."

"And your siblings?"

"I have two older sisters. They care about the climate crisis and what I'm doing. They're old enough to vote so can help that way."

"One sister was also trained by Al Gore," Cathy says, "and has done a lot of presentations and outreach events with me."

"I've known about climate change forever, basically," Sophia says. "Like, when I was little, I learned about how carbon dioxide caused problems, and how we breathed it out. So sometimes I would hold my breath. That was kind of funny. It's because I grew up in a family that cared deeply for the environment. Especially my grandfather, Daddu, being an IPCC climate scientist."

"That's pretty amazing. What does that mean—Daddu?"

"It's Punjabi for 'my dad's dad.' They call him the grandfather of composting."

"He was very big on carbon sequestration," Cathy says. "Locking carbon in the ground. That was his area of scientific expertise."

"Forgive me," I say. "Is this the grandfather who's been ailing?"

"Yes," Cathy says. "He passed away last week."

This news chokes me up and I discover I can't speak for a moment. None of us can.

"I'm sorry to hear about your grandfather, Sophia. But it sounds like his spirit lives on in the work you're doing. Was he a big inspiration for you?"

"He really did inspire me because he was an IPCC scientist. He's part of the reason my main message is: Listen to the experts and start acting on what they say! Because lots of scientists like him have done the research. They've proved climate breakdown is real, and they're telling us what to do. We just need to *listen* to them and *act*."

"There's one more layer to this story," says Cathy. "Another IPCC scientist showed up at the funeral of Sophia's grandfather. He talked with us about his frustration over the lack of action since the first big climate change report over twenty-five years ago. He said people don't really listen to scientists."

Sophia is part of a global climate action movement that, in September 2019, drew millions of youth in 150 countries into the streets to raise their voices for positive change.

"Back then," Sophia says, "lots of people were putting lies out there. Scientists doing real research were cut off. They had trouble publishing their results."

"Sophia heard this first-hand from her grandfather," says her mother. "This IPCC scientist at his funeral was saying the same things. He was really frustrated. But then Sophia talked to him, and he was *so* heartened when he heard about the work of his friend's granddaughter. He was very happy to meet her. You could see it on his face. He gave Sophia a big climate change hug. It was beautiful!"

THE GRETA EFFECT

They call it the Greta Effect.

Climate issues have jumped to the front burner of European election campaigns, with Green parties doubling their votes. Politicians everywhere are waking up to a new sense of responsibility—and guilt—for their lack of action to combat climate change. Record numbers of travelers in Germany and Sweden are saying "no" to flying and "yes" to trains. Millions of young people around the world are marching in the streets to fight for their future. And school attendance from Montreal to Melbourne, Dublin to Dubai, is showing a peculiar dip every Friday.

It all started on August 20, 2018, the day fifteen-year-old Swedish climate activist, Greta Thunberg, sat alone outside the Parliament House building in Stockholm, carrying a crude, hand-painted sign that read, *Skolstrejk För Klimatet*— School Strike For Climate Change. Her demand was simple but firm. She would end her school strike when the Swedish government got serious about slashing carbon emissions.

"Greta the Great"

Years of anxiety and fear over the impacts of climate change, and the lack of action by adults, had led Greta to give up hope for her future. "I overthink," she told a British journalist. "Some people can just let things go, but I can't, especially if there's something that worries me or makes me sad." Never being much of a talker due to her autism—she self-identifies as a "selective mute"—twelve-year-old Greta withdrew into a paralyzing depression and stopped going to school.

Her parents took good care of her and she started talking again, spilling out her worries to them. She showed them videos about climate change. They read books on it together. Her parents listened. They changed. They lowered their carbon footprint. Her father became a vegetarian. Her mother, a famous opera singer, stopped flying. Greta's depression gradually dissolved when she realized she could make a difference.

On August 20, 2018, after a record-busting heatwave in northern Europe, and fires ravaging Sweden's forests as far north as the Arctic Circle, Greta decided it was time to do something. She painted her sign, rode her bike past her school, and sat down in front of the Swedish Parliament House.

This exceptionally bright but painfully introverted nobody could not have imagined that, from Day One of her school strike, she would trigger a global climate movement, "Fridays for Future," that would energize young people—and shame adults—like never before.

"She changed us," her father says, "and now she is changing a great many other people. There was no hint of this in her childhood. It's unbelievable. If this can happen, anything can happen."

One of her teachers calls Greta a troublemaker. "She is not listening to adults. But we are heading full speed for a catastrophe, and in this situation, the only reasonable thing is to be unreasonable."

On Friday, March 15, 2019, a jaw-dropping 1.6 million students in 133 countries skipped school to march in a colossal climate strike inspired by Greta. And the walkouts continue, with youth around the world united by the *#FridaysForFuture* and *#YouthStrike4Climate* hashtags.

Not long ago, Greta was the kid at the back of the class who never spoke. She says that her selective mutism meant she talked only when she really needed to. "Now is one of those moments," she declared in a TED Talk viewed by millions. "Now I am speaking to the whole world."

And Sophia Mathur is listening.

> "**A**dults keep saying: 'We owe it to the young people to give them hope.' But I don't want your hope. I want you to panic. I want you to feel the fear I feel every day. And then I want you to act. I want you to act as you would in a crisis. I want you to act as if our house is on fire. Because it is."
>
> – Greta Thunberg

"Isn't it amazing, Sophia?" I say. "Here we are talking the day after Greta Thunberg made it to the cover of *TIME* magazine. I'm curious about your relationship with Greta and how she inspired you to follow in her footsteps."

"My mom bumped into her at a conference in Europe. Greta immediately knew who I was when my mom mentioned me. She's really inspiring, really brave. I honestly do think the youth movement she started is going to change how adults see the climate crisis."

"Some call Greta the best news yet for fighting climate change. Do you agree?"

"Yep! We've known about this issue for forty years but only now are people actually waking up to the reality. Greta has a lot to do with that. I don't know her personally, but I try to keep updated on what she's doing, what she's saying, how she operates."

"How did it all begin for you?"

"Last summer, I saw a video of Greta striking in Sweden. Her words were so perfect, so powerful, so *amazing*. She said adults weren't doing enough for climate change. That made me want to strike in Sudbury."

"I'll never forget Sophia watching Greta's video," says Cathy. "She looked up at me and said, 'Wow, Mom! Can I strike, too?' And I said, 'Oh, we better talk to your dad about that.'"

"I wanted to start striking right away, for the whole school year. But all I got from my parents was a 'maybe.' It took me till October to get them to say 'yes.'"

"How did you swing that?"

"In October, we went lobbying on Parliament Hill, about climate change, obviously."

"It was an emergency debate in the House of Commons," Cathy explains. "IPCC had just released an urgent report calling for drastic cuts in emissions within the next eleven years, or risk unstoppable climate change. Sophia could see that politicians were just not listening, and she complained about it. I realized how much she truly cared. By the time we got home, she'd convinced me that, yeah, we've got to join Greta."

"So I did it!" Sophia exclaims. "Our first school strike, in solidarity with Greta."

"Part of the equation here," Cathy says, "is that Sophia was the first kid in the Americas to follow Greta and begin school strikes. That was on Friday, November 2nd, 2018. Greta got to know Sophia on Twitter the next day."

Like Greta's world premiere strike three months earlier, not many people joined Sophia that first day in Sudbury's Memorial Park—a small group of adults and just two of her friends.

"Lots of my friends were actually begging their parents to join but they wouldn't let them miss school."

The local media told Sophia's mother that they wouldn't come back next time "unless you make it big." So she told them, "Okay. We'll make it big!" She tapped into her vast network of climate change allies and got nine *cities* to strike the next month. In Sudbury, over sixty people showed up, including two politicians, for a rally in minus-20-degree weather."

"I've been striking once a month ever since," Sophia proudly tells me.

"We are here, we are loud, because you are stealing our future. For way too long, the politicians and the people in power have gotten away with not doing anything to fight the climate crisis. But we will make sure that they will not get away with it any longer."

– Greta Thunberg

NUTS AND BOLTS

"How do you launch a strike? Give me the nuts and bolts of what you do."

"There's really three types of actions," Sophia says. "First, there's the actual *strike*. I usually say, 'Grab a sign and get out there!'"

"Where exactly?"

"Go sit somewhere, like in front of your school, City Hall, or a public park. The first Friday of the month I strike all day, talking to people and handing out pamphlets. We always do something big on those days. Like next month, I'll be striking in Washington."

"Wow! You're reaching out farther and farther. It's not all about Sudbury."

"My action is not just focused on Sudbury, or even Canada. I want to help save the entire world."

"I get that. So, what do you do the other Fridays?"

"I hand out pamphlets before school and at recess to get kids to help with some local activity, like signing a petition to get City Hall to declare a climate emergency in Sudbury. Or lobbying the hospital to raise awareness about the health impacts of climate breakdown. We do our own press releases, make videos, and talk to the media whenever we can. They seem to be listening."

"What would a climate change emergency declaration mean for Sudbury?"

"Over two thousand adults and kids signed our petition, so there's lots of interest. The motion is going to City Hall soon, and I really hope it goes through. It's a great way to raise awareness and make the climate crisis something they'll have to think about in all their decisions. Any time a city or a country declares a climate emergency, it makes me happy because it convinces the rest of the world they need to act.

"Besides Sudbury, my friends and I lobbied politicians on Parliament Hill about declaring a climate emergency in Canada. At least three political parties have already agreed with us. I'm proud that Canada is headed the right way." (Prime Minister Trudeau officially declared a national climate emergency just weeks after my interview with Sophia.)

"Amazing. So, *lobbying* is another important device in your activist toolkit."

"Yep. We meet with actual politicians to tell them our future is at stake, to get them to listen to climate experts, and push them to action."

➤ *On a recent lobbying campaign to Ottawa's Parliament Hill*

"It's funny," Cathy says. "The children are like magnets for politicians. They'll line up to talk to them."

"Just like Greta," I say. "So, what's the third kind of action you do?"

"A *rally*. That's a lot more work. Like on May 3rd, 2019 when we got over four hundred people to walk in a forest of birch trees. We called it a 'Fridays For Future Rally.' The idea was to walk for our future, to show the world that Sudbury is full of climate champions who want to make a better future for children. It took a bunch of meetings to put that together."

"We had a steering committee of seventeen people," Cathy explains. "Adults, kids, university students. We met five times between December and May. Sophia is learning how to be a good committee member."

"An important skill in your business," I say.

"Yep."

"It was part of a Canada-wide event," Cathy says. "The U.S. and Australia joined us. Canada had the most strikes of the three countries. We had 98 events across the country."

"Incredible. And in many ways, Sophia, it started with you?"

"It started with Greta," her mom says. "Sophia was the catalyst to get it going over here."

"Awesome."

"Tell Jamie about what you do *in* school."

"Not a lot of parents agree with their kids skipping school, so we have this other thing, where you wear a green bandana to school, or anything green, so people know they can talk to you about the climate crisis."

"This is instead of striking?"

"It's not striking in school but educating in school. Obviously, I'm not a teacher, but I can talk to other kids, my teachers, and my principal about the climate crisis and what they can do."

"Even the principal?"

"For sure! Like, before our big climate rally in May, I

actually convinced the principal to let all the Grade 4 to 6 kids out for the whole day."

"We really work hard to make our events fun and family-friendly," Cathy says. "That way, schools can feel comfortable joining. We don't want anything negative, like signs with swearing on them. We've got kids whose parents were born in Egypt, China, India—children from all walks of life."

"Sounds like good branding. Sophia, you mentioned that parents, including your own, aren't instantly supportive. What about other obstacles to striking?"

"Certainly, missing school is one, because lots of parents are super strict about marks. I think that's why my parents were initially weird about it. A lot of people think that striking and the other stuff we do causes us to miss out on our education. True, we might miss the odd math class, but I think we're learning a lot about public speaking, organizing, storytelling, making announcements—things you don't learn in school. We're learning about freedom of speech."

"How do you deal with skeptics who say you're just taking a day off school?"

"I sometimes get these negative comments when I'm striking. But I say, 'No, that's not why. I skip school because my *life* is at risk.' I really like school. But I also want a safe future, and I can't vote for the next two elections. I can't choose the people who will bring the change we need. So, we have to do it ourselves. Strikes are like our way of voting."

"How do you build the fun factor into such a serious topic?"

"Striking, rallies—they're fun because you get to hang out with people who have the same feelings as you. When I go to rallies, I get really excited. I scream my head off. I scream my speeches. I get super excited and super pumped. And we

Sophia (R) and fellow activists dance for climate action.

get to do a lot of activities together like singing, chanting, art, dance."

"Dance?"

"We actually created a dance to this song, 'We don't have time,' by Adam Baptiste of Sustainable Soundtrack."

"You actually get people up and dancing?"

"On our May 3rd rally, we got four hundred people dancing. When I went down to Toronto, I got people dancing there, too."

"So, you teach them all the moves?"

"It's a participatory dance so it's actually pretty easy. [*Screech!*] Sorry . . . Bella, calm down."

"Who's that?"

"Grizabella, named after one of the famous musical *Cats*."

"That's cool how your love of dance has leaked into your passion for this cause."

"A lot of people also bring their passion for *art* to this cause, including some really beautiful signs or amazing pamphlets. And there's Parachutes for the Planet."

"That sounds like fun."

"It is."

"It's a global movement," explains Cathy, "where kids create their own parachutes."

"They're not real parachutes," says Sophia. "Just a big round cloth. We decorate them to say kids want a soft landing on planet Earth when it comes to the climate crisis. My friends and I took ours to lobby on Parliament Hill."

"Sophia created the first one in Canada. There's been over a thousand made worldwide. Each one is a unique creation expressing the child's local concerns and hopes for the future. It's a beautiful project."

"Do you ever feel your activism is stealing your childhood? What about the other fun stuff twelve-year-olds can do?"

"Well, just this Tuesday was Track and Field, but I decided to go lobby on Parliament Hill instead, even though I did join a club to practice. Track and Field is a big deal that only comes once a year. But we only have a few years to act on the climate crisis. Track and Field will probably go on forever."

"So long as we have a liveable planet," I say.

"Right. Another example is we have these PA days—Professional Activity days, when the teachers go to school

Parachutes for the Planet created by Sophia and friends

Sophia (above Y in Sudbury) and friends show off one of their favorite Parachutes for the Planet.

but we don't. I've sacrificed many of those for our Fridays for Future meetings with my friends.

"When I have to miss school for other activities, I don't think my marks suffer. But we have a really big Grade 6 provincial test in Ontario, and if you miss a lot of school, it's hard to get good marks on that."

"You're going to be fine," says her mother.

"My teachers are happy about what I'm doing. I've got full support from my school, so I'm not worried."

"We demand the world decision-makers listen to the experts and take responsibility to solve this crisis. The youth have risen! The youth have risen! The youth have risen!"

Sophia leading a public climate rally at Queen's Park, Toronto

CRACKS OF FEAR, SLIVERS OF HOPE

"What would it take for you to call the strikes off, to shut down the rallies, to stop pounding on the doors of Parliament?"

"That's very simple. I'll be satisfied when adults see that it's us kids who will be most impacted by the climate crisis and do whatever they can to save our future. I'll be satisfied when politicians start listening to the climate experts and acting on their advice. Until then, we'll keep striking."

"Sometimes climate change can seem a little unreal. What have you personally experienced that keeps you motivated?"

"How about my house almost collapsing from an unbelievable snow load."

"What? Tell me about that."

"This spring we had tons of thawing and freezing. That made piles of ice on our roofs. Some homes actually collapsed. Luckily, we saw the first big cracks in our house."

"Where?"

"In *my* room! I went to lie down and looked up and I'm, like, 'No, this can't be happening!' There's this huge crack near the wall and a square bulge on the ceiling, like something's about to fall through. I got really scared and didn't want to sleep there. We were told we had, like, three hours to evacuate. It was that dangerous."

"Was this a freak thing that just happened to your place?"

"A lot of homes were seriously damaged," Cathy says. "We were probably in the top ten of damage."

"Do you think this disaster was caused by the very thing we're talking about—the climate crisis?"

"We had *thirteen* feet of snow this winter!" Cathy says. "And it rained twice in February. I'm sorry, it does not rain in the middle of winter. I've been up here twenty years. My parents are from the north. This does not happen."

"It's a shocking story. I'm glad you're safe. So where are you living now?"

"In a hotel near my school."

"Wait. You're in a hotel as we speak?"

"Yep. We actually have a cat, so it's kind of hard to be here with her." Sophia laughs. "She mews a lot but, luckily, she's found a place to sleep and isn't so annoying."

"We'll be here a while," Cathy says. "The whole roof needs replacing, and probably the entire front wall of the house. We've got insurance but some neighbors weren't so lucky."

"I've seen other scary stuff," Sophia says, "Like last summer, my friends and I were out paddle-boarding, having a whole bunch of fun, when we're called off the lake because of tornado warnings. I'm not saying that every tornado, every natural disaster is climate change. But you don't go to Sudbury for tornado-watching. And the next day we got *another* tornado warning. Later that summer there were forest fires all over, including one just fifty kilometers from town. We were at our cottage and could see and smell the smoke. It was terrifying. I don't want to move away from here, lose my home, the place where I grew up, all the trees we've planted. I don't want to lose all that."

"We discussed the rising danger of forest fires at a recent Fridays for Future meeting," Cathy says, "and I think it traumatizes the kids, even just to talk about it."

"What is it that scares you most about the climate crisis, Sophia?"

"Dying, basically. Because it's going to be such a big catastrophe if adults don't do anything. We're already seeing it. Not just weird winters and tornado warnings, but droughts, heat waves, hurricanes, floods. All that's going to affect us kids. So when I strike, I mean what I say. Because I feel like if I don't do anything, then our lives are gone."

"That brings me to the question of hope. Greta says that she will be more hopeful only when global emissions go down. What about you, Sophia? Are you more hopeful than when you started?"

"I'm hopeful that someday I'll live in a world where I am not afraid of dying because of the climate crisis. I get really hopeful when I see more and more youth striking. You don't usually have kids saying we need to act on climate change. And it's having an impact. I feel like more adults care. That's really empowering."

"What's it like to be part of a movement where there are millions of kids like you hitting the streets?"

"You feel like you're not alone. You're connected. We all share ideas. We have similar personalities. You learn you don't have to feel helpless or hopeless about climate breakdown. You feel like you *can* change the world. It's actually pretty amazing to be part of this global movement. And anyone can join."

Sophia and friends are all smiles after Sudbury City Council declares a climate emergency to promote more local positive action.

Two weeks after chatting with Sophia, my heart jumps when I discover this headline in the *Sudbury Star*: "City Council unanimously declares climate emergency."

"They did it!" I shout to my computer.

The photo shows Sophia and friends tossing an Earth ball above one of her Parachutes for the Planet, decorated with colorful flags and drawings of children from around the world. The article refers to "twelve-year-old Sophia Mathur who spearheaded the local Fridays for Future movement." A petition supporting the climate emergency declaration "that she helped inspire" was presented to City councilors. Their declaration concludes, "Be it resolved that the City of Greater Sudbury reaffirms action on climate change as a strategic priority."

Sophia (far left) and millions of like-minded youth have the whole world in their hands. "But don't forget the fun stuff!" says Sophia.

Digging deeper into the news feed, I discover a video clip of happy, hopeful interviews filmed at City Hall right after the successful vote. I laugh out loud near the end of the video when I spot Sophia, dancing victoriously across the screen.

> *"As Greta Thunberg said, we have not come here to beg politicians for change. We have come here to show them that change is coming!"*

Sophia made the headlines again in November 2019 when she and six other young activists launched a lawsuit against Ontario's Premier Doug Ford for slacking off on climate change targets. "He is not doing enough to protect our future and it's just unacceptable." Go Sophia!

TRAILBLAZER TIPS
....

Push adults to action
We don't know all the science or solutions. But we do know we'll be most affected by climate breakdown. Remind adults of that. Tell them to listen to the climate experts and take action.

Stay positive
A lot of people think of the minuses of the climate crisis and get depressed, angry, or scared. But I like to think of the plus side of the action we're doing together. Celebrate your victories.

Don't forget the fun stuff
Big issues in the past like civil rights, women's rights, or the peace movement have been helped by art, music, songs, and dance. They can help the climate movement, too. And it's a lot of fun!

Expand your circles
Talk to your parents about the climate crisis and what they can do. Talk to your wider family, your teachers, and principal. Soon you'll be talking with politicians. And don't forget the media.

Stand up! Speak up! Act up!
If kids want a future, we can't just sit around and do nothing. We have voices. We must stand up for our future. We must speak up. We must lead others—especially adults—to positive action.

Do your own homework
The media can spread lies to parents. Kids grow up believing those lies. If they are climate deniers, you'll never know how your future is threatened by inaction. Do your own climate change homework.

Start or join a movement

When I heard that my future was at risk, I got really worried. But I also had hope that if I did something, and maybe started a movement in my city, it could make a difference. It has!

"Ian is Mr. Great Bear—someone I look up
to as a hero."

– Norm Hann, teacher and paddle-board activist

IAN McALLISTER

Defender of The Rainforest
Telling stories that need to be told

Home: Denny Island, British Columbia
Pursuits: Award-winning nature writer,
photographer, and filmmaker

I feel like I've snagged an elusive halibut when I finally get Ian McAllister on the phone in his remote island home on B.C.'s rugged northwest coast. I happen to know that it took another writer two years to pin him down for an interview. With restless dogs barking in the background, and a silent countdown to his next field trip later that day, I dive right in. I've been moved by sampling his jaw-dropping books and online videos about B.C.'s endangered rainforests. I'm keen to learn about a world that few Canadians had ever heard about, until Ian made saving it his life's work.

SETTING SAIL
••••••••••••••••••

"What comes to mind, Ian, when you think of the shaping influences that made you the guy you are today, doing what you do?"

"I grew up in Victoria close to the water, and at a very young age—maybe thirteen, fourteen—we used to take off in this little open sailboat and go to the islands on these extended trips."

"What kind of sailboat?"

"I had this friend who'd built it as sort of a family project, a folding, plywood dinghy, kind of like a schooner." Ian laughs. "It was a really interesting boat. A bunch of us would just load it up and off we'd go. We didn't even have an engine, so we'd sail from island to island, camping around, catching fish, and just living on the beaches. Even though we were pretty close to Victoria and the Gulf Islands, at that time it seemed like we were in the middle of the South Pacific in the 1800's. It was pretty amazing."

➤ *Young Ian off on another adult-free sailing adventure*

Even before these adventures, Ian and his four siblings had been "dragged out" by their seagoing parents to some of the wildest parts of Vancouver Island, while still in diapers. "My parents were quite active, and we used to do a lot of exploring, trapping, hiking, and sailing along the rugged west coast."

In high school, Ian took his love of sailing up and down that coast to the decks of the *Robertson II*, sister ship to the famous *Bluenose* stamped on every Canadian dime. "It was a tall ship run by the SALT Society."

"What's that about?"

"It stands for Sea And Life Training. It's a pretty amazing organization that puts young people on these tall ships to learn seamanship and life-training skills. I remember, on that school trip, sitting on board the *Robertson II*, realizing I was totally hooked on the kind of seafaring life that we still live today.

➤ *An accomplished scuba diver in his early teens*

"I think that world just got in my blood at a very young, formative time. It left an imprint that still feels very strong, and I've been exploring that coast and trying to protect it ever since."

You could have pinched young Ian anywhere and B.C.'s wild west coast would leak out. Still would. Like he says, it runs in his blood.

JOINING THE FRONTLINES

In the summer of 1988, seventeen-year-old Ian and his father sailed to Clayoquot Sound, near the village of Tofino on Vancouver Island's windswept western shore. In those days, looking down on this area from a satellite, you would have seen a narrow, island-studded inlet rimmed by deep green forests, hemmed in by lifeless squares of naked earth—the telltale signs of industrial loggers homing in on some of the planet's biggest trees. On the ground you'd discover a

Industrial logging encroaches on old growth forest.

Protest at Clayoquot Sound

dripping, moss-draped forest, inhabited by cedars a thousand years old and spruce trees as high as skyscrapers.

Ian and his father had come to join a protest.

The idea was to draw the world's attention to the brutality of unchecked logging that was mowing down the area's temperate rainforests. But when they floated into the bay where the protesters were supposedly blocking a logging road, they realized that they'd missed the boat.

Most of the protesters had been arrested the day before. All the locals fighting to protect this natural treasure and native homeland—First Nations leaders, business folk, tourist operators—had been rounded up, herded onto an RCMP floatplane, and whisked away to face charges in a Vancouver courtroom. By the end of this fight, over 900 people had been hauled away by police.

Ian's father took stock of the rainforest glory around him, and the unfinished logging road that would destroy it, and came up with Plan B. He announced to the handful of remaining protestors that he'd take over the blockade, then proudly volunteered his teenage son for the most dangerous piece of the action.

Ian grabbed a book he'd been reading, climbed into a giant wicker basket, and got winched high into a towering tree. He was left dangling over the half-built road, high above the blast site.

Road construction ground to a halt. The loggers were stumped.

"Was that kind of a pivotal experience for you?" I ask Ian. "I mean, dangling up there in that basket?"

"Oh, absolutely. And to be inspired by so many people— First Nations, business leaders, other environmentalists. But back then, the environmental movement was very, very, new to B.C. In those days, timber was king. The idea of actually opposing the big logging companies was unheard of. It was all untested waters, and I think both the provincial and federal governments were truly shocked that anyone would question the industrial model of the day. So, yeah, it was quite combative and emotional, with lots of uncertainty. But it was empowering. It really felt like the right thing to do, and I think history has proven on all accounts that it was."

"I heard you were actually shot at up there in your basket. Is that true?"

Ian laughs. "The road-building crew would show up once in a while to see if my basket was still there, to see if we'd all been arrested and hauled off to jail. I think it was a pellet gun they were shooting. I tried to hide behind my thick

Margaret Atwood novel, but I don't think it offered a whole lot of protection.

"This happened a bunch of years before the really big protests. So that was my first introduction to frontline activism. Things got heated up pretty quick after that."

Luckily the pellets didn't leave a mark, but that experience up in the tree sure did.

"Where did you find your inspiration in your teen years?" I ask Ian. "Was it from other people?"

"My father, absolutely. He always had a love of wild places and he worked on environmental issues with the Sierra Club and other non-profits. So he certainly had a big influence. Both my parents did, really."

"Anyone else?"

"At Clayoquot Sound, I met Adrian Dorst and Mark Hobson, probably the two people who inspired me most in those early days, because they were doing exactly what I dreamed of. Adrian was a photographer, living out of an inflatable zodiac boat and just living the dream. He was a great naturalist and birder, spending lots of time out there, publishing books and doing incredible work."

"And Mark Hobson?"

"Same thing. He lived in Tofino on a little houseboat where he'd do his amazing paintings. He was also a photographer. Here were two guys that had found a way to eke out a living, doing great work, but also got to spend all this time in the wild. It was an incredible lifestyle."

It wasn't long before Ian bought his own zodiac. "I got pretty set on the west coast, you know, the really wild, rugged, dirt-ridden, gnarly ancient forest coast, and I just wanted to spend as much time exploring it as possible."

Exploring old growth forests and wetlands along Vancouver Island's wild west shore

WAR IN THE WOODS

Clayoquot Sound would be the first of a long string of front-line blockades for Ian, who, like his father, did whatever he could to protect the most precious gems of Vancouver Island's ancient forests.

Tree climbing became one of Ian's specialties.

"We were sort of roaming around Vancouver Island, becoming quite adept at climbing trees and bringing attention to its endangered forests. I did a lot of rough climbing initially, but then we spent a lot of time training. We'd climb trees, spend multiple days up there, then safely rappel down. We even designed systems where we could climb from tree to tree while still up in the canopy."

Early in their campaigns, Ian made a discovery that gave them a winning edge. "One thing we figured out was that the police couldn't climb trees very well," he says, laughing. "Eventually the RCMP got trained and started sending in their own tree climbers. But they really couldn't catch us. And of course, they couldn't cut the trees down when we were up there. So, yeah, we spent a lot of time in trees."

"Such heart-wrenching issues you were working on," I say, "but there was some fun in it?"

"Oh, yeah, but what we were doing was absolutely necessary. Anyone who chose to engage in civil disobedience couldn't take that lightly. It was a very serious issue that could have lifelong impacts. On the other hand, we did have a lot of fun. It was an exciting time. It really was."

When not swinging from tree to tree, Ian spent a lot of time studying maps showing the fast-shrinking forests of his beloved Vancouver Island. "The Sierra Club produced maps

Unchecked logging on Vancouver Island

of the island's old-growth forests. That's when I realized that less than twenty percent of these ancient, productive forests were intact. This was thirty-odd years ago and virtually nothing was protected. The B.C. government's stated intent was to protect only five percent of the entire island. We knew that was totally inadequate."

Ian came to believe more and more in the rightness of their peaceful acts of civil disobedience. "There didn't seem to be any alternative, other than to go stand on the frontlines and, at the very least, witness what was happening, document it, and spread the word. We felt empowered to be doing something about the gross ecological injustices inflicted on those ancient forests. We were always amazed by what we accomplished."

I ask Ian about another unusual tool in his protest kit: a Kryptonite bike lock.

Ian laughs. "That's quite a story!"

The story began on October 18, 1990, when the forestry goliath, MacMillan Bloedel, began clear-cutting along the Tsitika River valley in what one conservation group called "a virtual declaration of environmental war." Located on Vancouver Island's remote northeast coast, this untouched valley sheltered a unique killer whale (or orca) habitat— Robson Bight—famous for its one-of-a-kind whale-rubbing beaches.

To this day, no one knows for sure why killer whales keep coming back here to rub their bellies on the beach's wave-washed pebbles. Maybe for a cool massage? A fun place to play with other family groups? Whatever the reason, biologists knew even back then that these particular beaches are an extremely sensitive staging area for large numbers of these endangered whales.

Spy-hopping killer whale checks out life above the sea.

And so, the logging company was about to punch a logging road into those beaches when Ian and his friends showed up with a couple of bike locks. He parked his van on the one and only bridge over the Tsitika River, climbed under the van, and locked his neck to the undercarriage.

"Everything else had been done. Letters had been written, studies had been done, and it just didn't matter. It was all falling on deaf ears. In those days, timber companies ruled everything in this province. So that was our way to kind of blow up the logging operation. I gave my friend Dan the keys to the Kryptonite locks, but he panicked and threw them in the river."

My jaw drops at this point in Ian's story. "Why did a so-called friend throw your keys in the river?"

Ian laughs. "He just panicked. I don't know what happened. And so, they had to cut my van apart to get me out of there."

"What sort of tools did they use?"

"Some kind of big diamond drill that sent all these sparks flying in my face. Then my jacket lit on fire, so they took a fire extinguisher and shoved it in my face and let it go. When they finally pulled me out of there, I looked like hell."

"Who's actually doing the cutting?

"Yeah, that's the funny thing. The RCMP just sort of deputized the loggers, and so they got under there and did the police's job for them."

"What about the bike locks?"

"They basically took the van apart, but they didn't actually cut the locks. So I ended up having to walk around Courtney for three days with those Kryptonite locks around my neck. Those were crazy times."

➤ RCMP handcuff Ian (still wearing bike lock) after cutting him out from under his van.

With the Internet and cellphones still years away, Ian's zany stunt still managed to attract media attention around the world. "In those days, so much of what was happening was out of sight, out of mind. People didn't know about it. Very few got out to see what was happening. Our ability to communicate was much more limited. So I figured it was the only way this story could be told."

Ian had figured right. "Our blockade, all that media coverage, actually stopped the road. Today it's a protected area. There's quite a few examples like that."

Just out of high school, with loads of successful conservation campaigns already under his belt, Ian was learning the power of *story* to capture the world's attention and help protect the places he loved.

The stormy eye of Vancouver Island's protests circled back to Clayoquot Sound in 1993, peaking that August. This was "the really big protest" that Ian had told me about, going down in Canadian history as the largest act of civil disobedience ever. Almost a thousand protesters would be arrested before that fiery summer ended. What became known as "The War in the Woods" stole headlines across Canada and beyond.

"Clayoquot Sound ultimately got protected. If the community of Tofino and local First Nations hadn't had the foresight to stand out on that road, the place would've probably been destroyed. Today there's over a million tourists that go to the Tofino area every year and, of course, the reason they go there is because of the natural environment—the protected rainforest, the scenic coastline, the intact ecosystems."

Even as the bulldozers went silent and the last protestors hugged each other over their victory, Ian's sights had swung from his Vancouver Island home to a bigger, wilder conservation target: a mist-shrouded wonderland along B.C.'s north shore.

Ian, his father (on dock), and friends prepare to set sail.

LAND OF THE SPIRIT BEAR

When Ian was in his early twenties, his father, Peter McAllister, organized an ocean voyage to the Koeye River (*"K'way"*), a two-day sail from the north tip of Vancouver Island. Set in a spectacular rainforest valley, this area was said to be full of salmon and pristine white-sand beaches, heavily tracked by grizzlies and wolves. Peter had chartered a three-masted schooner and invited along bear biologists, photographers, journalists, and environmentalists to help uncover the valley's secrets and share them with the world. Ian was lucky enough to squeeze on board.

At that time, Ian had never seen a grizzly bear and knew next to nothing about photography. But one evening, as he sat on a driftwood log, wriggling his toes in a beach crisscrossed with grizzly prints, and staring out to the open ocean, he felt something shift inside. He knew from that moment on that he would devote himself to "tracking that shy monarch of the rainforest, the maker of those great tracks," and learn how their fates were intertwined.

"That first fateful trip into the Koeye taught me two things: that a river valley truly can change a person's life forever—and that I had better buy a camera."

Fueling Ian's new sense of urgency to protect the Great Bear Rainforest was the dire fact that the Koeye, along with many of the hundred-odd wild river valleys strung across the region, were slated for industrial logging. That winter, Ian and his new wife Karen collected virtually all the forest and wildlife information available on these valleys—*and barely filled a shoebox.* They discovered that no one had done even a basic biological survey of that coastline, yet huge swaths of it were destined to be clear-cut— basically mowed down by chain saws—"a decision that would deface the wild raincoast landscape forever."

Ian and Karen pause along the Great Bear trail.

One night, after staring long and hard at maps of the region spread out across the floor, Ian, his dad, Karen, and other green-minded friends founded the Raincoast Conservation Society and began to think big.

They planned a systematic aerial survey of all the intact river valleys from one end of the Great Bear Rainforest to the other—a distance of 400 kilometers (250 miles)—all the way to the Alaska border.

Their plans took flight the next summer, thanks to some serious fundraising and a Society member's floatplane equipped with a wing-mounted video camera. They flew up and down every valley along the coast, amassing an invaluable library of video footage as well as on-board still shots captured by Ian's sophisticated new camera.

Ian and Karen returned the next summer, now in their own trimaran sailboat—the *Companion*—which they had sailed from Lake Ontario, through the St Lawrence River, down the east coast of the United States, then through the Panama Canal, and up the west coast, sometimes navigating by placemats, stars, or good old skipper's luck. For summer after summer, the *Companion* served as their floating home and research station. Their goal was to explore all the valleys they'd documented from the air, checking out bear and wolf populations along the way.

By the spring of 1996, Ian and Karen had met their goal, pulling anchor at the mouth of the final river valley on their list. They joyfully trimmed their sails and steered south to their new home on Denny Island, population 138, nestled in the heart of the Great Bear Rainforest. It was there that they put the finishing touches on their first coffee table book that was jam-packed with jaw-dropping photos of wild coasts, mountains, and animals—including the ghostly white "Spirit Bear," the fabled icon of this extraordinary place. Released to global acclaim in 1997, they called it *The Great Bear Rainforest—Canada's Forgotten Coast*. It was to be the first of many books, beautifully written and visually adorned, to make you fall in love with what *National Geographic* called "The Wildest Place in North America" and, hopefully, add your voice to its defence.

So began Ian's journey as a world-class visual storyteller, applying all his blossoming skills as a photographer, writer, and naturalist to celebrate and protect his adopted home.

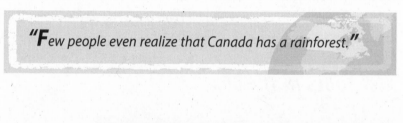

"Few people even realize that Canada has a rainforest."

Black bear cub with spirit bear sibling

Ian endures a rainforest deluge to capture its beauty on film.

NEW TOOLS IN THE BOX

Fast forward to the 20-teens.

Ian has become a mighty conservation force to be reckoned with. He has another five award-winning books under his belt, on everything from wolves to whales, all showcasing the Great Bear Rainforest. For his efforts in fighting for this area, he's been honored as a "Kickass Canadian," a *Globe and Mail* "Highly accomplished Canadian," and one of *TIME*'s "Leaders of the 21st Century."

By this time, Ian and Karen had founded their own environmental organization, Pacific Wild (pacificwild.org), dedicated to "defending wildlife and their habitat on Canada's Pacific coast." Powered by a crackerjack team blending natural science, indigenous culture, visual arts, and public outreach, Pacific Wild was hugely instrumental in ushering in a province-wide ban on trophy hunts for grizzlies. "It took a long time to get a full ban on trophy hunting," Ian reflects. "Almost non-stop campaigning and presentations and videos. We used every tool in the box, year after year, to finally realize it."

Ian's arsenal of conservation tools is now pretty slick, including one of the coolest and most powerful storytelling tools on the market: a camera-mounted drone.

I admitted to Ian that the kid in me gets a real charge out of the work he does with drones. "I heard you launched a drone from your sailboat to spy on some shady gold mine. What was that about?"

"We'd heard rumors of a toxic tailing spill on Banks Island, south of Prince Rupert, so we sailed all the way up there. When we visited the mining camp, they refused us entry. So, we went back to the boat and sailed around to another inlet. We realized we could just fly our drone over this big ridge and get right on top of the mine. What we saw was just horrendous. The entire tailings pond had overflowed into a salmon river. We managed to get video footage of salmon jumping out of the water, right where the tailings pond had burst and totally destroyed this river."

"What did you do with the footage?"

"We managed to sail through the night to a place that had satellite Internet. We uploaded the videos and it went nationwide. It hit CBC's *The National* that night, and the mine got shut down about a week later. It hasn't opened since."

"Wow!"

"Yeah, it's quite unprecedented. But it was all because of a bit of drone technology. Otherwise, we would have sailed away without any idea of what happened."

Ian's toolkit got a major upgrade in 2016 when, after years of fundraising, he began work on his biggest project yet: the giant screen movie, *Great Bear Rainforest—Land of the Spirit Bear*. For this job, Ian hired a specially trained drone pilot to fly a jumbo octocopter, nicknamed the "Beast" capable of slinging a twenty-pound, $100,000 IMAX camera up and over mountains, or getting up close and personal with a breaching whale.

Ian feels this film, released three years later, pushes the envelope in the world of wildlife filmmaking. "We're doing everything we can, from documenting it above and below water, using 360 VR (visual reality) cameras, IMAX cameras, aerial drone work, on-the-ground field imagery. We're trying to document this incredible natural history from as many sites and angles and perspectives as possible to tell the whole story."

Telling that story was not without its dangers.

"We spent a considerable amount of time diving every day, especially in the cold winter months when the water's so clear. The hard part is, winter months bring the most challenging weather." Once, while peacefully filming a mob of playful sea lions deep underwater, Ian broke the surface to face blinding, sub-zero winds. "We just barely got back to the boat before the storm hit."

Another hair-raising challenge was trying to capture Spirit Bears catching salmon as the fish leapt up a waterfall. Getting his camera in just the right position to capture this unique behavior sometimes left Ian hanging by a rope over a torrent of bone-crushing whitewater, within striking distance of a bear's claws.

The results, he says, were always worth the risks.

Ian gets up close and personal with a fishing spirit bear.

"Visual storytelling has always been a really important part of our conservation work. At the heart of it, what we were really trying to do was capture these stories and tell them in ways that compel people to take action."

ECSTASY AND AGONY

In 1990, when Ian first set sail for the Great Bear Rainforest, the whole place was designated as a Timber Supply Area, basically a free-for-all playground for industrial loggers. Back then, few people outside of its borders even knew it existed. Even fewer knew of the First Nations people whose culture and livelihood have depended on it for over ten thousand years.

It took twenty-six years to flip that picture on its head—recasting this area from an unknown economic breadbasket, ripe for pillaging, to a globally renowned natural treasure and Indigenous homeland. Ian was there through it all, with one firm hand on the tiller, and the other on his camera, giving his adopted home a thorough makeover in the public eye.

For Ian, 2016 was a banner year.

Premier Christy Clark kicked off the good news on February 1st by lifting the curtain on an awesome new poster to promote preservation of the Great Bear Rainforest. She was happy to announce that five dollars of every poster sale would go to a trust intended to do just that. The poster celebrates a hard-fought agreement, over a quarter-century in the making—hammered out by First Nations, the B.C. government, environmental groups, and forest companies—to set aside one-third of the Great Bear Rainforest as fully protected conservation areas and to permanently protect 85% of its old-growth rainforests from industrial logging.

The poster features a shining Spirit Bear, made popular by Ian's breathtaking photos and videos, nimbly poised on a slick rock, in the middle of a swirling salmon stream, looking utterly at home. Below the bear is a Proclamation:

> *"Conserving one-quarter of the world's*
> *coastal temperate rainforest.*
> *British Columbia's Great Bear Rainforest,*
> *our gift to the world."*

Soon after announcing this historic agreement, the B.C. government and their First Nations partners unveiled a set of hard-hitting management plans to protect the marine environment along the Great Bear coastline. The feds followed suit with a firm commitment to protect a good chunk of the coastal seabed through a system of marine parks and special management zones.

The magnificence of the Great Bear Rainforest, and the high level of protection it now enjoyed, captured the royal gaze of Queen Elizabeth II, whose family has always had a warm spot for exotic conservation projects. On September 26th of the same year, her grandson, Prince Harry and his duchess wife Meghan, hopped on a floatplane to Bella Bella on their B.C.–Yukon tour. Their mission: to officially admit the Great Bear Rainforest into the Queen's Commonwealth Canopy—kind of a hall of fame for globally significant forests meant to last forever. The idea of this royal badge of honor is to encourage 2.3 billion citizens, in 53 Commonwealth countries, to take better care of their forests.

Can't hurt.

By the fall of 2016, thanks to this deluge of provincial, federal, and international attention, and Ian's IMAX film project literally taking off, things were looking pretty rosy for safeguarding the wild wealth of the Great Bear Rainforest.

But when it comes to conservation, Ian would be the first to tell you: "Never let your guard down!"

The crash came on October 13, less than three weeks after Harry and Meghan flew back to Buckingham Palace.

It happened on a dark and stormy night.

Really.

It was past midnight when a Texan tugboat, pushing a barge from Alaska to Vancouver, entered the narrow Seaforth

Black bear scoops a salmon from a rushing river—another of Ian's jaw-dropping images that captured world attention.

Channel, part of the Inside Passage, which is especially busy with marine traffic when the weather is lousy. At thirty meters long, this tugboat was carrying a hefty payload of diesel fuel. But it wasn't quite long enough to require a local pilot to climb on board and navigate through those tricky waters.

At 1:00 AM, the captain, who some reports say was asleep at the wheel, slammed blindly into a reef, sinking his ship and spilling more than 100,000 liters of diesel—a whole train car's worth—into the cool, clear waters rimming the Great Bear Rainforest.

By the next morning, a purple-yellow slick coated the water and beaches around the spill site, including a prime clam and fishing area used by the Heiltsuk First Nation. That afternoon, fisheries officers imposed a ban on all harvesting in the area so nobody would get poisoned.

All this happened a dozen kilometers west of Bella Bella, almost within sight of Ian's home on Denny Island.

The shoddy clean-up response that followed was roundly condemned by the Heiltsuk, Premier Clark—even Prime Minister Trudeau, who called it "inadequate" and "unacceptable."

Trudeau turned up in B.C. a month later to unveil not another pretty poster, but a $1.5 billion coastal protection plan to prevent such ecological disasters from happening and, if they do, to do a much better job cleaning them up. "It's time for a change," he announced.

Change is indeed in the wind for the Great Bear Rainforest and its convoluted coastline, but maybe not the kind Trudeau was referring to.

"**P**eople around the world are concerned about introducing Big Oil to the west coast of Canada. We shouldn't put Canada's Pacific coast at risk, just to feed more cars in Shanghai with our dirty oil. That just doesn't make sense."

PIPELINE THROUGH PARADISE

The sinking of that Texan tugboat, and the pathetic job at cleaning up the mess (you still can't fish there), happened as the Northern Gateway pipeline proposal was ripping across national headlines. If approved, this project spelled a quantum leap in tanker traffic through marine waters skirting the Great

Bear Rainforest. Not surprisingly, a lot of people, who now cared deeply about this region, were sorely steamed.

Not since the "War in the Woods" had B.C.'s environmental community galvanized around an issue with such passion and power. And now they were protesting shoulder to shoulder with Indigenous leaders, local businesses, like-minded politicians, and a rising tide of concerned citizens.

Of course, Ian joined them on the front lines. But this time he didn't rely on baskets or bike locks to make his point. Instead he applied his well-honed skills as a visual storyteller to fire his message around the world.

Take, for example, Pacific Wild's video called *Pipeline Through Paradise*. Posted on YouTube (check it out), this punchy thirty-second clip is full of Ian's typically lavish aerial and in-your-face photography of misty mountains and beguiling bears, plus some heart-stabbing facts about the millions and millions of liters of crude oil already spilled into B.C.'s coastal waters *before* any new pipelines. The video ends with the clarion call, "Say NO to the Enbridge Northern Gateway pipeline."

Soon after the oil spill near Ian's home, Prime Minister Trudeau joined the rising chorus of naysayers. "The Great Bear Rainforest is no place for a pipeline," he told reporters at a packed press conference in Victoria. "It is a jewel of Canada's west coast."

Maybe he was inspired by Ian's video?

With the Northern Gateway project permanently shelved, Ian still worries about other looming megaprojects that could ramp up tanker traffic along the Inside Passage. "Everything is at stake with this energy issue, and it has come to us squarely in the fight to keep oil and gas tankers out of the fragile waters of the Great Bear Rainforest."

Ian's heightened concerns about impacts to the marine environment—wild salmon, whales, and herring are already in trouble—are reflected in his new focus, literally, on the area's near-shore environment. "It just seemed like a natural progression to try to look at the ocean with a subsurface lens and, of course, to look from the ocean back to the rainforest."

One of Ian's favorite photos is of a wolf wading into the sea toward his camera, its legs below the surface, its eyes just above it, focused squarely on him. The wolf is hunting for herring eggs laid on seaweed near the shore. Ian had been stalking this shot for years, after watching that particular wolf

Wolf wading into the sea—a photo that Ian stalked for years

pack over many seasons. "That's the kind of marine image I'd really hoped for—the ocean and the rainforest, the wolves, the herring, all in one picture."

That unique photo, stitching together the precious ecosystems Ian has fought so hard to protect, ended up on the front cover of *National Geographic* magazine in editions around the world.

In February 2019, Ian released his latest gift to the world, the IMAX blockbuster, with his signature call to action. "The film gives viewers a glimpse of how precious, but also how fragile the Great Bear Rainforest is. It shows the richness, both ecologically and culturally, of the rainforest, and it will, hopefully, also inspire public participation in its protection."

THE ADVENTURE CONTINUES

Ian has made it his life's work to protect the Great Bear Rainforest, where he lives, works, and plays. For this intrepid storyteller, it is home. "In this world of diminishing ecological returns, I get a lot of fulfillment just being here. It is hard to describe how special this place is. If we just leave it alone and stop treating it like an inexhaustible resource, it will have a fighting chance. I love it up here. I've raised my kids up here. There's still so many things left to do and places to explore."

As our interview wound down, Ian told me that a week earlier, he and Karen and their teenage son and daughter were sailing past the whale-rubbing beaches of Robson Bight where, decades earlier, he had U-locked his neck to the undercarriage of his van to stop a logging road. "We saw a whale blow and went over to have a look and discovered it was a sperm whale, the first known sperm whale on the B.C. coast since 1984."

"Wow."

"Yeah, it was amazing. My kids got to see a sperm whale. I'd never seen one on this coast. That was super cool!"

> **"I** think we are just so fortunate to have a place that still has the working parts—the full suite of flora and fauna—and we're not talking about, 'How are we going to bring these animals back?' And, 'How are we going to restore this system that's been destroyed?' which is really the ecological conversation for most other places. Here, we just have to protect what we have.**"**

TRAILBLAZER TIPS
....

Tell a visual story
I've always taken pictures from a young age, worked on films, books, articles. People respond more viscerally and earnestly through visual storytelling than perhaps any other medium.

Never give up
If we just give up, if there's greater complacency, we'll be spiraling in a bad way that much quicker. Never give up, whether it's protecting a local place or some big environmental issue.

Spread the word
If you see an ecological injustice, witness what's happening, document it, and spread the word.

Do whatever you can
It can be heartbreaking to think that we are entering a very fragile, uncertain time on this planet. Let this awareness empower you to do whatever you can to make things better.

You don't have to be an "environmentalist"
Don't get pigeonholed into thinking, I have to be an environmentalist. At Pacific Wild we need engineers, mariners, I.T. experts, storytellers, photographers, writers. Everyone has a different way to help. Stick with what you love and you'll find a way to make it work for the environment.

Use online tools

The technology platforms available to young people are far greater than ever before. It's amazing how they're using these for creative engagement, inspiration, and public education.

Beware of advice

Don't take too much advice. Trust your instincts. Most of the things we've achieved have been done in spite of the advice that we got.

"Elizabeth May is a tireless and dedicated leader who is devoted to creating a more supportive and equitable society . . . It's inspiring to see such an astute and passionate environmental advocate who actually walks the talk."

— Sonia Wesche, Geography Professor, University of Ottawa

"Without her passionate voice for the Earth on Parliament Hill, green politics are much more likely to fade to black. If only this woman were our Prime Minister!"

— Adria Vasil, Author of *Ecoholic*

"Elizabeth May is a fighter—and one to be reckoned with, as a number of major international industries and Canadian governments have come to realize."

— Farley Mowat, Author and environmentalist

"Her work goes beyond the typical environmental issues to deal with the most pressing social and economic issues facing Canadians . . . Canada is a better place as a result of Elizabeth's brave and determined leadership, and would be even greater if we only listened to her wise council more often."

— Josh Snider, Youth sustainability leader

ELIZABETH MAY

Extraordinary Activist

Fighting for change, one campaign at a time

Home: Sidney, British Columbia
Pursuits: Environmentalist, author, lawyer, and
former Leader of the Federal Green Party

*What do others call Elizabeth May? "Canada's supreme warrior
princess, a true Canadian hero, a beacon of leadership . . ."
I could fill a page. What does she call herself? "A lawyer in
recovery, aspiring theologian, feminist, vegetarian, writer, cook,
sister, daughter, single mother, grandmother, campaigner, activist,
citizen." Once I finally got through to her in her Parliament
Hill office, I might have added to that list, "everybody's sister."
That's how I felt. She was so instantly warm and attentive,
talking to me, this total stranger from Yellowknife. She even
apologized for eating her lunch during our interview. We were
in fact born just months apart. We have experienced this planet
over the same decades, though few have defended it and loved
it like she has.*

BORN CRUSADER

Elizabeth May is about to be born.

It's June 9, 1954, Hartford, Connecticut. Her mother is feeding nickels into a radio attached to her hospital bed. Already well into the labor of birthing a child, she does not want to miss the climax of a drawn-out public hearing examining Senator Joseph McCarthy's claims that Russian spies have infiltrated the U.S. government.

And so, Elizabeth makes her world debut, bathed in a turbulent stream of political newscasts.

A wooden angel hung over her crib at home, "but a mushroom cloud would have been more appropriate," Elizabeth writes in her autobiography, *Who We Are*. Like all children of the Cold War fifties, she was tucked in each night under the looming shadow of nuclear annihilation. Little did baby Elizabeth know that her mother was doing everything in her power to stop those nasty H-bombs from harming her daughter.

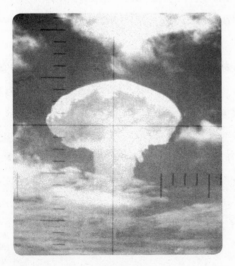

➤ *Elizabeth's mother fought atmospheric testing of nuclear weapons, like this 1962 blast seen through the periscope of a U.S. submarine.*

As Elizabeth tossed away her diapers, learned to walk, and eventually talk, her mother stole what time she could to hit the streets, the radio, and community halls to fight against the atmospheric testing of nuclear weapons. As a new mother, she was painfully aware of warnings that radioactive fallout, from exploding nuclear warheads in the sky, could multiply the risk of childhood leukemia. She would later take her campaign to the highest authority in the land—and win.

When Elizabeth was still a toddler, it seems that something of her mother's activism had already rubbed off. Or was she genetically predisposed to be an activist? Or maybe influenced by past lives?

I ask Elizabeth for her take on this mystery. "You once told Farley Mowat that you were 'born with an environmental consciousness.' How so?"

"From my earliest years, it was always there," Elizabeth tells me. "My mother remembers when I was about two, I told her I hated airplanes. She thought that was odd because I'd never been in one. I told her I didn't like them because they scratched the sky—and they *do* scratch the sky. They damage the atmosphere. I was absolutely right. So that's clearly a very early stage of environmental consciousness. Where does that come from? I don't know."

By the time Elizabeth was five years old, she was conducting her own campaigns—in the schoolyard. Although her mother tried not to infect her with nuclear anxiety, Elizabeth had already plugged into her concerns. She often warned her kindergarten classmates not to eat snow, insisting that it was contaminated with strontium-90 from radioactive fallout.

"This did not make me popular," Elizabeth reflects.

Her mother's activism led other parents at Elizabeth's school to label her a Communist. So, Elizabeth and her younger brother Geoffrey were often banned from class parties and "mostly ostracized" the rest of the time. In Elizabeth's autobiography, her brother still describes that phase, from nursery school to Grade 9, as a time when they lived as "prisoners of conscience."

But this was also an idyllic phase of Elizabeth's life, grounded by the small family farm where she grew up.

REFUGE
....

"Tell me about your first home, your family life."

"I was fortunate to grow up in a very beautiful location, a kind of a paradise, really. We lived on seven acres in rural Connecticut with dogs, cats, ponies, sheep, chickens, and an extremely obstinate donkey. There was also a rich wetland area with lots of snakes. My mom had built a swimming pool to be as natural as possible. She fooled the ducks and they often landed there. So I grew up with lots of animals."

"What were your favorite activities as a kid?"

"We were very happy just to be home in our own place, with our own woods, with our own animals. A lot of what my family did involved just being outdoors. We really enjoyed each other's company, so on Sunday afternoons we'd go for long walks. We'd get out our walking sticks and go out for a couple of hours together. My dad, who was raised in England, used to enjoy coming back for high tea, a kind of British tradition of having boiled eggs and other breakfasty things for dinner. It was always a fun thing to do on weekends."

➤ *Elizabeth and her "extremely obstinate donkey"*

"What did you and your friends like to do?"

"We were in a very remote area so none of my school friends lived anywhere nearby. But other friends would come over to play at our place or jump in the swimming pool on a hot summer day. We had a tremendous tree house in an old gnarled willow tree that my dad built for us. The woods were an almost inexhaustible source of adventure. We were so fortunate to have a lot of natural space and a lovely yard to play in. Our place was a constant beehive of activity."

"You said you had ponies. Would you go riding?"

"We'd take the ponies out for rides on trails through the woods in back of our place. We also had a lovely carriage that a pony could pull. That was also fun. But I was just as happy to sit in the barn and talk to my ponies, rather than putting a saddle on them and going for a ride."

"Lovely. You've got me thinking about *Charlotte's Web.*"

"Definitely apropos. I loved *Charlotte's Web.* E. B. White was a brilliant writer and arguably one of the very earliest environmental writers for kids. He had a unique sensibility for ecosystems and nature. I identified with the opening scene where the girl, Fern, runs into the house because the runt pig is about to be killed. One of the things that happened, being so close to my animals, was, first, I stopped eating lamb. Then, by the time I was ten, I stopped eating any meat at all."

"So, of all the childhood factors that shaped your chosen path, which do you think were most influential?"

"My mom, my dad, my brother were the biggest factors. My pony, my dog, the animals I lived with and loved. My close relationships with the humans and non-humans in my childhood—that was huge. Of course, my sense of closeness with the natural world meant that I did care a lot about environmental issues, even before they were called that."

As much as Elizabeth enjoyed her family refuge, she also journeyed far afield on some interesting adventures, usually at the side of her megaphone-toting mom. "Mostly we were homebodies, but we would often join my mom's campaigns, going to demonstrations, working against nuclear weapons testing, going to Washington to picket the White House. We did those sorts of things together, which is kind of unusual for a family.

"Even when I was a very tiny child, I was very much a supporter of my mom and her work as an activist. I respected enormously the difference she was making. I understood, because she explained it to me, the work she was doing to end nuclear weapons testing. She was a volunteer, a housewife, and a mom. But unlike other moms, she was spending tons of time giving speeches, distributing petitions, and going to Washington to lobby."

And it looks like the right people got the message.

Elizabeth well remembers that summer day in 1963 when

U.S. President John F. Kennedy, along with representatives from Britain and the Soviet Union, signed the Nuclear Test Ban Treaty. "I had a very early experience of individual citizens acting together—particularly my mom—as part of a larger movement for positive change. That was a pretty empowering lesson in democracy and had a big influence on me."

Here's Elizabeth, already steeped in world-changing activism, and she's only just celebrated her ninth birthday!

> *"What makes me believe that one person can change the world? My mom. Because she did. I aspire to be someone who makes a huge difference in Canada."*

LIKE MOTHER, LIKE DAUGHTER

Over the next couple of years, Elizabeth became actively engaged in new issues that her mother was fighting for. "The civil rights movement and then the Vietnam peace movement began to dominate our existence."

As passionate as eleven-year-old Elizabeth was about joining these fights, these still were, after all, her mother's issues. Elizabeth's deep dive into a more personal brand of activism was triggered by the tragic and mysterious circumstances surrounding the death of her sheep.

It started with two Easter presents—one baby lamb for her, one for her little brother Geoffrey. Black faced with white woolly bodies, Smokey and Baaa were warmly welcomed into the family. From the start, they were pets, not livestock, which sometimes drew out "cringeworthy comments" from neighbors and friends. "If you aren't going to eat them, what are they for?" one family friend asked. Eight-year-old Geoffrey managed to answer, "They are for . . . to love."

And love them they did, watching with joy as they frolicked across the grass.

➤ *Nursing one of her pet "lambies"*

When the lambs grew up, Elizabeth's father sent them back to their original flock to breed them, hoping for more lambs. They both came home pregnant, offering Elizabeth a perfect Grade 6 science project—to detail the gestation and birth of the next set of lambs, which they named Corey, Thunder, and Spring. "These new lambies were amazing. They came when they were called by name, as smart as any dogs we'd ever had."

Until they started dying.

Baaa was the first to go.

She became violently ill, convulsing, twitching, thrashing. "The symptoms were just horrific. We asked the local vet to do an autopsy to see if she'd eaten something poisonous. The vet couldn't see anything. We couldn't figure it out."

Then Thunder and Spring developed the same symptoms. "The harrowing trip to the vet was repeated twice. Their eyes rolled back in their heads and they frothed at the mouth as I tried to tell them I loved them and they'd be okay."

Which they weren't. Mother Baaa and two of the three new lambs died a horrible death.

A couple of years later, when Elizabeth was in middle school, she figured it out. She read Rachel Carson's *Silent Spring* and learned about pesticides poisoning sheep in Arizona. "Rachel Carson could have been describing my own lambs. The symptoms exactly matched how my own sheep had died."

Trying to stay calm after this shocking discovery, she wrote a letter to the nearby town of Bloomfield to see if they had sprayed pesticides along their road in the months before her sheep died. They wrote back, saying they'd sprayed malathion and methoxychlor in those very ditches. Elizabeth shuddered, knowing these were chemical cousins from a family of lethal nerve gases developed during World War II. "I wrote back and told them, 'You killed my sheep,' and that was the end of the conversation.

"The effect of all of this was that I became aware that I was now an environmentalist and knew what I wanted to do with my life. I would go to university and become an environmental lawyer."

While waiting for those university doors to open, Elizabeth found lots of causes to fight for and networks to join. "I signed on with environmental groups like Friends of the Earth and Sierra Club. I got all their newsletters. I started a file on pesticides. I got involved with a lot of issues, basically starting with my mom's, then growing into my own. And my mom would help me with my issues."

When Elizabeth entered high school in the late 1960s, supersonic transport planes—or SST's—were big news. Their glittering promise of lightning speeds for globetrotting passengers was soiled by their many potential impacts on the environment—which grabbed Elizabeth's attention. She decided it was time for a frank chat about SST's with a powerful man named Lowell Weicker, their local U.S. Senator.

"I remember I was only a kid. I mean, my mom had to drive me to the meeting. I didn't have a driver's license. I talked to him about blocking any U.S. government money for the SST because of scientists' concerns about supersonic transport damaging the ozone layer. So there I was, a teenager, already involved in ozone issues, helping to stop the spread of harmful SST's. Then, imagine that years later, I ended up helping to negotiate the Montreal Protocol, a global ban on ozone-depleting substances."

Ozone-depleting Concorde SST

That's Elizabeth: ahead of the curve.

The next big issue that she took aim at was banning the use of throwaway soda pop bottles and cans. "I wrote a piece of legislation when I was in high school, by adapting a Bill that Oregon had just passed, to ban single-use beverage containers. There were no deposits in those days. It was all just garbage. So I brought that Bill to the Connecticut Senate. I went to hearings on it. My mom told her friends to come because they thought no one would show up. Of course, all the big lawyers from Coke and Pepsi showed up. They had to get a bigger hearing room. All these people came to say what a terrible idea it was to pass this Bill. It took years, but finally the Bill did pass."

"You're a teenager, taking on big government, big business. That's incredible."

"It never occurred to me that I couldn't write a Bill, introduce it at the State level, and get it passed. But that's just a tribute to my upbringing. I'd always been encouraged to believe you can do absolutely anything if you're prepared to put the energy into it. You can get government to do what you want. You just have to explain it properly."

"Making the impossible possible. That's what you do."

"Yes, but at the time, I didn't think it was impossible. I thought things were easy to fix."

"Besides your mother, were there others who really inspired you to take such bold action?"

"My mother was no doubt the biggest influence on me as a child. She showed me what one person can do to try and change the world. But as I got older, I have to say that one of my real heroes was Senator Eugene McCarthy." (Not to be confused with Joseph McCarthy, the hunter of Russian spies, whose voice Elizabeth heard at the moment of her birth.) "Eugene opposed the Vietnam war and was running for the Democratic presidential nomination. He was just an amazingly brilliant, inspirational, and wonderful man. It really became hero worship for me. He was a very big feature in my life as a kid. I worked as a volunteer on his campaign. That's why I went to the Chicago Democratic convention in August 1968. I'd just turned fourteen. That was certainly my first time getting tear-gassed."

"What? Tear-gassed? Tell me that story."

"Everybody there was tear-gassed if you were in the peace movement. My mom went there as a delegate for Eugene McCarthy. She was allowed to bring a family member with her, so she brought me along to see democracy in action. It never occurred to her that I would get tear-gassed and potentially beaten with police clubs. The Commission that later investigated the event concluded that this was a police riot aimed at anyone in Chicago who was against the war in Vietnam.

"This was very disturbing for a kid who'd never doubted that if you're in trouble, you go to a policeman. I'd been raised that way. But once, my mom and I and some other kids were walking back from the convention, looking for a place to eat. It was late at night and we were scared. My mother said, 'Don't worry, kids. We'll be fine as long as we don't see a policeman.' That definitely had a lasting impact on me."

"What did you take away from that experience?"

"It's not that I stopped liking police. But my Chicago experience certainly shaped how I think about democracy. I recognized that democracy is quite fragile. It's not a constant state. It requires a 'degree of vigilance' as Thomas Jefferson said. I watched the power of a democratic state being used to oppress people just because of their beliefs. I learned that fascism can take over a country of nice people. I'm not saying that happened in the United States in 1968. But I am aware that it can happen anywhere, even Canada."

Elizabeth returned to her high school in Hartford, Connecticut, more pumped than ever to change the world. "In Grade 10, I started an environment club at our school. Then I started the Environmental Action Regional Task force of Hartford, or EARTH. I contacted thirty-five other high schools, and we formed a coalition to do environmental work to get ready for the first Earth Day in April 1970. When I changed schools in Grade 11, I started another environmental club. I set up a lending library of environmental books in one corner of the science lab."

"I have this image of you as a teenager, debating with government and industry big shots, just nailing them with facts. How did you get your fingers on all the information needed for your many campaigns?"

"I'd always had a lot of intellectual curiosity to go look things up, check things out, find the right book to tell me the things I wanted to know. I learned that from my mom. She would write quotes from Nobel Laureates on little index cards, so she was always prepared to push back when someone said she was an uninformed, emotional woman who didn't know anything. I learned early that, if you're going to campaign on issues, you have to be well buttressed by facts, preferably by published scientists, preferably by men, or you won't be believed as a young woman."

"Sure, but with the Internet still decades away, how did you access these scientific data from your remote farm?"

Elizabeth learned the importance of thorough research— and so much more—from her mother (L).

"I subscribed to *Environment* magazine put out by the Scientists' Institute for Public Information. That was a very useful source of information. Very, very helpful."

"This was a regular publication that came to your mailbox and you'd devour it?"

"Exactly. It was written for lay people but it was serious science. I remember an issue about something called 'acid rain.' I first read about it there and I remember thinking, *Oh my gosh, what's acid rain?*"

"What about your special interest in pesticides?"

"The magazine offered a very detailed five-booklet series on pesticides, so naturally I ordered the whole thing. Of course, we had a regular library near our home. There were other places I could go for information. But mostly I'd send money through the snail-mail. It wasn't that hard. I mean, I simply did what I could to get the information I needed to put a good case together. So I built up quite a box of files on pesticides."

By the time Elizabeth finished high school she was already steeped in world-changing activism.

As committed as Elizabeth and her family were to saving the world in so many ways, they were not immune to issue fatigue.

It was time for a serious vacation.

"The rapidly escalating war in Southeast Asia, with its napalm and horror, remained the focus of our family life, until we took a summer vacation to Cape Breton Island in 1972." Elizabeth's parents fell in love with the island's beauty and tranquility, so far removed from the political turmoil plaguing the United States.

It was time to pack up and move.

Her parents decided that their beloved house in the country would sell faster if they threw all their furniture into the deal. Elizabeth had to leave many treasures behind. But luckily for the forests and animals and people of Cape Breton, she scooped up her heavy box of files on pesticides before walking out the door for the last time.

"My vision comes from an unusually political childhood, an activist upbringing, and a deep love of democracy. It comes from knowing that working together changes the world."

HARD TIMES

Elizabeth was still a teenager when her family claimed Cape Breton Island as their new home. Welcome to Margaree Harbour, a tiny village of forty-two souls on the island's rugged north shore. Full of hope for a quieter life in this postcard-perfect landscape, it never occurred to them that such a move could wipe them out financially. Nor did Elizabeth anticipate parachuting into a firestorm of environmental issues.

"When we moved to Cape Breton, it felt like my activism was going on a shelf because my family bought a restaurant business that was initially disastrous." They lived in a one-room log cabin beside the restaurant that, they soon discovered, was poorly chinked against the wild winter winds blowing off the sea ice. The snow screamed in between the logs and piled up in dark corners beyond reach of their next-to-useless barrel stove. The cabin leaked so badly that they had to wrap the whole thing in plastic, "to keep it fresh," jokes Elizabeth.

"It was hard, but I loved the land and I loved being in Canada."

Besides, Elizabeth would soon be going off to university to get that environmental law degree, right?

Wrong.

Well, actually, Elizabeth and all her new friends *did* make the trip to St. Francis Xavier University in Antigonish. But while signing up for classes, she learned she must pay $400 on the spot.

She phoned her dad.

Long pause at the other end.

He told her to take the bus home. They didn't have the money.

"Abandoning university was not part of the plan. I stayed home, waitressing and cooking in the summer, collecting unemployment insurance in the winter, so my parents could afford groceries, heat, and electricity."

Then, in the spring of 1975, along came the big pulp and paper companies with their planeloads of pesticides. They

Dumping a planeload of pesticides on a commercial forest

wanted to protect their forests from spruce budworm attack by spraying them with the same chemicals that had killed Elizabeth's sheep.

Elizabeth calmly rolled up her sleeves. She dusted off her big box of pesticide files. Her name was about to become a household word across Nova Scotia.

"I suddenly started working on the budworm campaign as a volunteer. With all the campaigning I'd done and information I had, I was able to write the fact sheet for a major petition against aerial spraying. This was back before Xerox machines, so we had to run them off on an old Gestetner machine in the basement of a local church. The technology of grassroots activism on Cape Breton Island in the mid-1970s was nothing like what we can do today!"

Elizabeth describes it as "an epic struggle" that often sapped every ounce of her energy. "Against all odds, we succeeded in protecting Cape Breton from aerial pesticide spraying."

Waitressing, cooking, campaigning, winning. So went the beat of Elizabeth's life for much of her twenties, until March

1980, when her dream to be an environmental lawyer once again took flight.

While taking in an International Women's Day concert in Sydney, Nova Scotia, she had a random conversation with a lawyer who knew of a special program to admit more women into law school—with or without an undergraduate degree. "It was a *tremendous* piece of luck that I even heard it was possible."

Thanks to Elizabeth's stellar marks in high school, her fame as a successful campaigner, plus a recommendation letter from the governor of Arkansas and future U.S. president, Bill Clinton (this young woman had connections, in this case, through her mother's life-long friendship with Clinton), she got accepted, with some hefty financial help to boot. "I can still remember the first time I was able to afford to go to a movie and the feeling of that movie ticket in my fingers as I stood in line."

Elizabeth, her daughter and mother visit U.S. president, Bill Clinton.

Elizabeth's joy in reading law, talking with her professors, and arguing legal points was rudely interrupted in her final year of law school by "the most personally punishing" environmental fight of her life. "Big Paper" was back, this time proposing to spray the deadly herbicide, Agent Orange, used to defoliate Vietnam, over the same forests Elizabeth had helped save from aerial pesticides. The idea was to kill all leafy trees in favor of coniferous ones to help boost Scott Paper's astronomical profits in making—guess what?—toilet paper!

Elizabeth threw herself into a scorching two-year court battle that cost her parents eighty acres of land they'd been saving for retirement. Elizabeth missed her graduation day from law school. She was busy cross-examining one of Big Paper's key witnesses.

In the end, despite heroic efforts, they lost the case. But thanks to the public attention it stirred up, and dwindling global supplies of this infamous chemical, the forests of Elizabeth's Cape Breton home were spared another massive aerial assault.

At 29, with countless campaigns already won and lost, and a law degree in hand, Elizabeth was a well-armed force to be reckoned with in Canada's surging environmental movement. "By then I had all the background, tools, and skills I needed to do the work I'm doing now."

She went on to fight successful campaigns in Nova Scotia to ban uranium mining and build public opposition to nuclear energy. She worked as a legal advocate for consumer, poverty, and environmental groups across Canada. She fought for Indigenous rights at home and in the Amazon. She worked as top adviser to federal Environment Minister Tom McMillan, helping to create national parks, new pollution laws, and the

Montreal Protocol that saved the ozone layer. As Executive Director of the Sierra Club of Canada from 1989 to 2006, she helped grow the organization from a kitchen table gathering to one of the country's most powerful voices for environmental sanity.

Somewhere in there, Elizabeth did a seventeen-day hunger strike, got arrested during a pipeline protest, wrote eight best-selling books, picked up four honorary degrees, and was named by *Newsweek* as "one of the world's most influential women."

And, oh yes, she kickstarted Canada's Green Party and proceeded to be its first leader elected to federal parliament.

Makes you wonder if those little lambs had anything to do with it.

Elizabeth May resigned as the Green Party leader on November 4, 2019 after helping to elect three Green MPs during that fall's federal election. "I'm very excited about this," she told reporters on Parliament Hill. "I wanted to choose a moment when we had a lot of success before leaving." After leading the party for 13 years and through four elections, she made it clear that she's not done yet. "I am not stopping my work. The climate crisis is as critical as ever."

> "**W**e need to wake up and smarten up. We do not lack solutions. We lack only the awareness of our situation, the courage to choose the right priorities, and the political will to embrace them."

FAITH, HOPE, AND CHARGING AHEAD

"I read somewhere that you sometimes work twenty-hour days, seven days a week. That's quite the personal sacrifice. Where do you get your energy, your inspiration?"

"One thing is just pure, dumb luck. I think we underrate how much we're just born with certain skills. I'm genetically programmed for optimism. There's no other way to put it.

"The other thing that sustains me is faith in a Creator. I happen to be an Anglican, but I could be Buddhist, Jewish, Hindu, or Muslim. I could be Sikh. My particular approach to faith is inclusive and non-judgmental. I have faith in powers beyond what we see in front of us. I don't want to get too

A leader with unshakable courage and conviction,
Elizabeth is arrested while supporting a peaceful
environmental protest in Burnaby, B.C.

theological, but to give an honest answer, I couldn't cope with
the political life I have now if I didn't believe in the power of
prayer, in the ability to recharge my batteries by focusing on
the larger questions, and in the value of being of service. My
faith helps me avoid getting too wrapped up in how I'm doing
personally, and whether people like me or not."

"I'm personally so grateful for that answer," I say.

"That's so sweet of you. Thank you."

"What advice do you have for empowering young people
to make a difference?"

"I'm genetically programmed for optimism."

"First, be very, very sure that *you* are important, that the world needs you. Don't allow yourself to be just observers or consumers, watching stuff happen. You're a citizen of Canada. You have a role. Even if you're ten years old, you have power."

"Second, if you're going to take on a tough issue, find like-minded friends, even if they're not campaigning with you. Secure yourself with people who love you, and you can love back. This will protect you and recharge your batteries. And if you can't find people, find a dog or cat to love."

Elizabeth's world has changed radically since the day her mother hung a wooden angel over her crib. The human population has soared from three billion to almost eight billion. The threat of catastrophic climate change has replaced the mushroom cloud. Denouncing environmentalists as threats to economic prosperity has replaced the anti-communist witch-hunts of the fifties.

"If we had a planetary health button on the dashboard of our cars, it would be flashing red."

Still, in the midst of these new and ominous shadows, Elizabeth refuses to lose hope.

"Being hopeful is not the same thing as being unrealistic," she writes in her autobiography. "This is not the dewy-eyed dreamy hope of the deluded. In the context of the climate crisis, hope is hard work." Here she quotes a professor friend of hers who says, "Hope is a verb with its sleeves rolled up."

Could there be a more fitting image of eco-warrior, Elizabeth May?

> "*The* situation may seem hopeless but it is not. We will change things if we believe we can. Strong, positive, and committed people are needed. Cynicism and despair are our enemies."

TRAILBLAZER TIPS
....

Embody optimism
I am an "operational optimist." We have no time for pessimists. We are out of time for procrastination. We really only have one way forward: to become active and save ourselves.

Tell them the good stuff
You cannot move people to change simply by railing against what's wrong. We need to move people to change by describing how much better it could be. Tell them what you're for.

Believe in the possible
I have so often been part of environmental campaigns against impossible odds. And so often, we have won. No campaign against impossible odds is ever impossible. Truly believe that.

Refuse to be intimidated
If you are told a subject is too technical or scientific for you to understand, don't believe it. You may not be an expert, but you can read and understand what experts say. Collect good expert quotes and unleash them if someone suggests you don't know anything.

Be creative
Every campaign has its own dynamic. Let your creative juices flow. Maybe satire will work for you. Maybe song. Any campaign will attract more people if you take an innovative approach.

Don't take "no" for an answer

If you want to meet some official in government or industry, call every day. Drop by the office and get to know the staff. Be persistent, but also unfailingly polite. You may be in this for the long haul, so don't burn any bridges.

Beware of burnout

Any campaign can take a physical and emotional toll. Take care of yourself. You'll need the support of friends and family. Build love into your campaigns.

Elizabeth and her husband, John Kidder, celebrate their marriage on Earth Day, 2019, trailed by a pod of giant orca whales. "We intend to be gloriously happy—and very Green!"

"It's not every day that someone as young as Ethan
has such a strong, positive influence on an entire city.
Ethan is a rare combination of a thinker and a doer."

– Ontario Nature

"Ethan has the tools and spirit to lead and inspire
generations to come. His work and future aspirations
are 100 percent buzzworthy!"

– Canada's Top 25 Environmentalists Under 25

"Young people have such a unique voice. Ethan sets
a really great example for fellow youth, who may
not feel like they can make a big difference."

– Sarah Hedges, Ontario Nature Youth Council

ETHAN ELLIOTT

Champion for Bees and Beyond
Finding a voice for the voiceless

Home: Stratford, Ontario
Pursuits: Environmental changemaker, youth advocate,
and Bee City Canada promoter

It takes me over two months to nail down an interview with bee warrior and youth advocate, Ethan Elliott. This is one busy activist, as you are about to find out. His good green deeds have earned him the honor of being one of Canada's "Top 25 Environmentalists Under 25" in 2017 and a "Top 30 Under 30 in Sustainability" award in 2018. On top of all that, he loves student politics, acting, climbing, and skiing—which is what he'd been doing just before I got him on the phone. He confessed he was a little beat from a "crazy, crazy week" ski instructing at Kitchener's Chicopee ski hill, where, as it happened, I learned to ski when I was Ethan's age. Before we dove in, he told me that he carries his activism with him, even onto the ski hill. Witnessing first-hand the decline of dependable winters in his region, he sees the prospect of not being able to ski as "a little terrifying."

THE PODIUM

He wasn't ready for this. No way. At thirteen, Ethan Elliott already had lots of experience helping fellow youth rise up and fight for a clean environment. But that was way back in Grade 5.

Nothing had prepared him for this.

You could see it in the way he rose from his chair, in the wobbly way he walked to the podium. His palms were sweating, his heart thumping. For someone who so desperately loved to be outside, he was suffocating in the stuffy Council chamber of the Stratford City Hall.

"I was in Grade 9," he tells me, during a two-hour phone interview from his Stratford home. "I'd kind of lost interest in environmental stuff for the block between Grade 5 and Grade 9. It was a long block," he says, laughing. "I wasn't as involved as I should have been. I guess I was just busy growing up."

Ethan's interest in things environmental flared up again working on the Suzuki Foundation's Blue Dot program, a campaign to get cities across Canada to guarantee their citizens the right to breathe fresh air, drink clean water, and eat healthy food. Ethan joined a grassroots movement lobbying Stratford to sign on. But the local movement had been losing steam. Ethan had popped into the meeting just to add his support.

"A lot of people had more or less given up on the whole Blue Dot idea. So they were happy to have some new energy in the movement—especially a young voice, because that was missing."

Little did Ethan know that, out of the blue, so to speak, he would be invited to pitch the idea to the bigwigs enthroned in Stratford's chandeliered Council chamber.

"It was terrifying for me being called up to speak in front of all those people. This was back before I'd become a lot more confident in my abilities in the environmental movement."

Looking back after several years, Ethan can't say exactly what happened up at that podium. Near the end of his sweaty spiel, he suddenly felt a surge of fresh nerve that lifted his head and sharpened his focus. "That was kind of a hurdle for me."

In the end, the bigwigs refused to sign on. "They supported the Blue Dot idea," remembers Ethan, "but it didn't end up passing."

Not that night, anyway.

It would take months of lobbying by other Blue Dot volunteers for Council to finally say "yes" to formally granting Stratfordians the right to fresh air, clean water, and healthy food—a green and glowing fuse lit by Ethan's brave talk. He knew that standing up at that podium had changed something inside him. "That was kind of the first time where I really sensed that my voice could turn into action."

RUNNING INTO THE WOODS

Ethan came by his love of nature naturally. With family roots reaching deep into the clay-rich Mennonite soils of southern Ontario, he craved being outside. "I really kind of had the whole outdoorsy upbringing. I was always in nature as a child."

➤ *Exploring the "big sandbox" of nature*

For his farming grandmother and great-grandmother, the land was their life and work. "I used to go outside with them and just stay out all day. We'd go to the woods and just kind of explore." Sometimes Ethan would bring friends along on his adventures in the woods, making forts, damming creeks, climbing trees, catching frogs. "We used to go out there and roam and run around. I liked how it was kind of like a big sandbox.

"As I got older, I wasn't so much of a run-into-the-woods kind of kid anymore." He started playing piano, soccer, and a bit of hockey. His passion for skiing caught fire. School ate up more of his time. But no matter how busy he was, just being outside remained a treat.

▲ *Bringing in the cows on his grandmother's farm*

➤ *A lover of snow, Ethan has been bombing down hills his whole life.*

IDLE-FREE ZONE

"When you were young," I ask Ethan, "were there any environmental issues that really grabbed your guts?"

I'm surprised by his laugh.

"I really wish I could say there were, but living in Stratford, it's really a bit of a bubble. The town's really great at protecting our wild spaces, so that's never been a huge issue here."

But issues in the wider world began niggling at Ethan. "I used to always be super aware of the environmental destruction I'd heard about from logging and anything to do with bulldozers and stuff like that. But I never really took action at that young age—with the exception of the idling campaign. That got me going."

"Tell me more."

"Back in Grade 5, I used to attend this monthly program called C.A.R.E. Junior, where you'd go plant gardens or learn about environmental issues. That's when I first heard about the impacts on people of idling cars. I became super passionate about idling, just understanding that *your* right to keep *your* car warm doesn't really beat out *my* right to have clean, healthy air. It really frustrated me. The exhaust as you walked in front of the school was unbearable. That kind of opened the whole environmental movement for me."

Ethan joined his school's environmental club and dove head-first into an anti-idling campaign. The kids made posters and put them up all over the place. They made an anti-idling video and showed it to school staff and the parent committee. They made signs to put on cars. They knew Stratford already had a five-minute-max idling bylaw, so they talked that up, too.

"Do you think you were successful?"

"I really think we did have an impact. People started making the link between the decision to idle their cars and the health of their kids. The issue became much more personal. That's where I learned how important it is to make those connections. You can't just tell

someone, 'Oh, this is hurting the trees!' No. You have to make a personal connection with their lives."

A FORK IN THE ROAD

Catapult Ethan through time, beyond the piano lessons, the soccer games, the misty middle-school years, the Blue Dot days, and he lands squarely on his feet beside a high school teacher who changed his life.

Kerry McManus's day job is teaching math and French at Ethan's high school, Stratford Central Secondary School. If she wore a superhero cape—which wouldn't surprise me— it would have the letters C.A.R.E. on the back, for Common Action for the Restoration of the Environment. This is the environmental group, co-founded and chaired by Kerry, which, back in Grade 5, lit Ethan's environmental fuse over the car idling mess at his elementary school. Since 2003, Kerry has led small armies of students into the environmental trenches on many fronts, from tree planting and river clean-ups, to organizing parties to celebrate Earth Day and Not-so-Scroogy Christmases. Did I mention that Kerry is also a Stratford City Councilor? Quite a powerhouse, this woman.

"It's ironic that she's now one of my teachers in high school," Ethan says. "She knew of my anti-idling interest from way back and told me about this opportunity to go to an Ontario Nature Youth Summit." Every September, over a hundred green-minded high school students from across Ontario gather at Geneva Park, a YMCA camp and "leadership center" on the wooded east shore of Lake Couchiching in the heart of Ontario's cottage country.

Kerry knew that Ethan would be a shoo-in.

But Ethan was stalling.

"She told me about the Youth Summit, like, a week and a half before it happened, and at first I didn't want to go. But some of my friends were like, 'Oh, my gosh, you should try this. Maybe it will do something!' My parents kind of pushed me, too."

For Ethan, this turned out to be a ginormous fork in the road. "I eventually ended up going and I realized after, that if I hadn't decided to go, I have no idea where I'd be today."

"Wow! So, carry on. What happened up there at Geneva Park?"

"It was just such an important weekend for me. The camp is on this stunningly beautiful waterfront. And the connections I made were incredible, all these passionate people working for the environment, doing everything they can to make a change. I just kind of got looped into this movement. It's an incredible program, and I credit Ontario Nature with pretty much rebuilding my interests and bringing me back outside."

Throughout our interview, Ethan kept steering back to the Youth Summit, calling it "a big wakeup call."

"I'd always loved being outside, but I'd never really connected it to making a change in the world until that weekend. It was kind of a lucky chance that I happened to go there. But I think it really shaped me into the person I am today."

Since then, Ethan has come to identify himself as an "Environmental Changemaker," a tag Kerry McManus could take some pride in.

And it turns out she wasn't finished with him yet.

Ethan joins a pack of passionate youth at Ontario Nature's 2018 Youth Summit Camp.

TAKING POWER

Soon after Ethan's awakening on the shore of Lake Couchiching, Kerry encouraged him to join her on the City's Energy and Environment Committee. With Kerry at the wheel, this group amounted to a large-diameter pipeline of green advice to the highest decision-making body in town—the Stratford City Council where, back in Grade 9, he'd delivered that first shaky presentation. Ethan was recruited as the one and only youth representative.

"I was only supposed to be on the committee for one year. Somehow, I've stuck around and here I am in my third term. This, too, has been really pivotal for me—understanding that I had a voice in such a direct way. I had a vote. I was able to propose motions that go right to City Council. In combination with the Youth Summit, this really got me super inspired about everything!"

The Summit also put Ethan on the radar of Sarah Hedges, Managing Director of Ontario Nature, who invited him to join their Youth Council, described as "a vibrant peer network promoting lasting, positive change through conservation action."

"Sarah is another incredible person that got me connected and moving on. She was *so* passionate about integrating youth and giving them a voice on environmental issues."

As passionate and committed as Ethan's fellow Youth Council members are, when they gather together from across the province two or three times a year, it's not all serious stuff.

"I remember last year we wanted to go snowshoeing. Trouble is, there was no snow." Was it climate change or just a weather thing? At that moment they couldn't care less. Instead, they slapped on their snowshoes and took off into the woods. "We were like, 'We're going snowshoeing, damn it!' I remember running around through the mud, falling all over the place, getting all muddy with our snowshoes on. We have some pretty crazy fun as a council. It's a great group of people."

Ethan is quick to include his mom and dad as part of his support team. "For sure, they've had a role in my environmental activism. They've always kind of asked me, like, 'How can you do more? How can you make a positive

With his kick-sledding buddies at a Youth Council camp

change in the world?' And their support through all this has been really instrumental in keeping my focus. But a lot of my activism I've pretty much done on my own through Ontario Nature."

BEE THE CHANGE

Google Ethan Elliott these days and you may discover him as "that bee guy," or a member of the "Bee team," or a star in a "Bee movie." And you might conclude that he's always had a thing for bugs, spiders, and bees.

Not so.

It was at one of those high-adrenaline Youth Council camps that Ethan first got the bug to throw himself on the bee bandwagon. He learned about an outfit called Bee City Canada that spreads awareness of the value of bees, and grants badges of honor to cities and schools that do their bit to protect them.

"To be brutally honest," Ethan admits, "when I started working with Bee City, I wasn't hugely passionate about bees and other pollinators. I didn't know too much about them. But then I was like, okay, this is about positive environmental change, so let's go!"

It took Ethan a while to come around to the importance of bees, and he quickly found that he wasn't alone. "It's been hard convincing people to care, because bees aren't necessarily an issue that resonates well with people. They kind of laugh it off with the 'Bee movie' meme. It's a bit of a joke. But people have to understand that the decline of bees and other pollinators is a huge issue that really does matter."

Ethan's initial attempts to get his home town designated as an official Bee City were met mostly with laughter, shrugs, or apathy. Certain media branded his supporters as hippies and tree-huggers.

◄ *Hamming it up with a swarm of bee friends*

In a way, you can't blame them. How many people really know or care about the importance of bees and their insect cousins? Important for *what*? How about pollinating over three-quarters of all plants on Earth—they just couldn't survive without insects. And we're not talking obscure plant species in a rainforest half a world away. One out of every three bites of food you eat got to your plate thanks to pollinators. Besides helping keep *us* alive, pollinators keep countless ecosystems healthy, which, in turn, clean the air we breathe, stabilize soils, support wildlife, and on and on.

Nobody knows this better than Ethan.

By beating the public awareness bushes and pulling the right levers among his wide and well-oiled connections— both on the environmental and political stages—Ethan

Planting yet another bee-friendly garden in a Stratford park

succeeded in getting Stratford officially designated as a Bee City, second only to the megalopolis of Toronto.

"I think that's been one of my biggest accomplishments—the change I've been able to make in my city. And the gardens we've planted. And the conversations we've started. I now hear Bee City come up in plenty of conversations around town. People are making the transition to more sustainable gardens. Being a Bee City is now a legitimate thing. I know plenty of people who didn't care about bees at all until I brought it up at City Council."

Ethan's initiative has changed the face of Stratford in subtle but significant ways. Take the Bruce Hotel, Stratford's luxury hot spot just steps away from the world-famous Shakespearian Festival Theatre. This one-of-a-kind hotel is surrounded by incredible flower gardens—bee food. Enjoy its fancy indoor pool and two restaurants. But please, no pets.

Unless you count honey bees. There are maybe seventy thousand of them in the hotel's backyard.

The Bruce bees, as they are affectionately known, live in half a dozen hives, managed by a beekeeping farmer. Except for one especially hot, dry summer day when the bees gathered round the swimming pool for a refreshing drink, people and bees are co-existing peacefully. The bees reinforce the hotel's eco-friendly practices. Honey from the hives is used in its specialty bakery. They even plan to set up a Bee-cam near the hives for the enjoyment and education of their well-heeled guests.

Other urban beehives, pollinator gardens, and public awareness campaigns are hitting the streets of Stratford. Good for bees, good for business, and good for raising the flag for an environmental issue that counts. And Ethan continues to lead the charge.

"In the end," he says, "I really learned how important bees are, and I think that my action kind of inspired other people, even other towns." Since Ethan's victory in Stratford, over thirty-five communities across Canada now wear the Bee City badge, undoubtedly a ball that he helped roll across the country. He calls it a "Bee City revolution."

And here Ethan's story takes a bizarre twist. "Ever since our designation went through, I unfortunately can't be on Stratford's Bee City committee."

"But why not?" I ask him. "After all you—"

"Because I'm not eighteen. City Hall says I'm too young to sit on that committee."

"That's crazy!"

"Uh-huh. I'm still involved with it, though. And I still organize garden plantings. I've done maybe four so far with more in the works."

"And what does that look like?"

"My role now is more as facilitator. I'm not an expert on pollinator plant species, even though I'd love to be. So, I pretty much find the funding and select the location and just show up to help organize the plantings." Ethan laughs. "I don't tend to design the gardens, because if I did, they'd all die!"

FROM BEES TO THE BULLRING

"So, what now?"

"I guess I've made climate change my main focus. And I've had to pursue other groups. Even started my own."

He calls it "Two Degrees." The name refers to the global temperature threshold, above which, the UN warns, earthlings may tip toward catastrophic climate change. Ethan started his group to help put the brakes on that slippery slide. And, not surprisingly, it is 100% powered by high-octane youth. "The whole idea is to inspire youth to take action on climate issues." Among the group's over thirty volunteers—and growing—no one's over the age of nineteen.

Scroll through the Two Degrees Facebook page and you can almost hear the shouting. "Time's up! Youth demand climate action . . . Join the Canadian youth movement to end climate change . . . Contribute to the fight!!"

Their page links you to the latest climate change headlines, youth-led petitions, and hard-hitting tips to "become a champion for your community and the environment!" It shows photos and videos of group members storming the streets, like slamming "mean tweets about climate change," or attending a premiere screening of former U.S. Vice President Al Gore's latest climate change movie, *An Inconvenient Sequel*, and engaging him in a post-film Q&A.

"My main goal is to safeguard our future for *us*, for youth. I don't want to harp on the older generation too much, but they kind of left us with a pretty bad hand. I think we need to play that hand aggressively and really make our voices heard. Otherwise, we're guaranteed to lose."

Ethan's sense of urgency is reflected in Two Degrees' catchy call to action—"*Fight like your future depends on it!*"— and the group's logo—an up-thrust fist rising against a blazing red sun.

"Ethan, what would you say is the hardest thing you've done in all your environmental work?"

"I think it was waking up to the fact that I really had a voice and shouldn't be afraid to make it heard. There's also the whole Two Degrees thing. It was a lot of work. But I learned

Leading a student-led climate rally in front of Stratford City Hall

a ton about delegating tasks, about leadership. Then there's the apathy."

"Apathy?"

"Yeah. It's such an issue among youth. They don't feel they have a voice. I see it every day. We'll be talking about some issue or a campaign we started, and someone's like, 'Oh, well, it doesn't matter what we say, they'll just make a decision anyway.' That may be true, but that doesn't mean we shouldn't take action." Ethan talks of a necessary chain of awakening among youth—from apathy to caring to knowledge to action. "Moving from apathy to action, that's the hardest part."

"But how do you get people to care?"

"You need to tell a story about *why* you care. Don't just say, 'Oh here's a polar bear, it's dying, it sucks.' Talk about why polar bears are important and who they're important to. Make a personal connection and people will care. I don't want to be critical of the environmental movement—it's fantastic!—but I think it can focus too much on the doom and gloom. Instead, talk about what's possible, what's positive. People resonate better with positivity than with negativity. That's how you really inspire caring and activism."

"What about personal sacrifices you've made along the way?"

"It's been a long road, but I don't think it's taken anything from me. It's really been enriching for me. And I think that I bring a relatively unique perspective, especially to youth."

As for the future, Ethan feels in some ways like he's only just begun. "I'm still relatively new to the environmental movement," he says, laughing. "I haven't done many things I'd love to do. Two Degrees represents a lot of that. That campaign is getting a lot more traction lately."

"For example?"

Celebrating Stratford's Bee City designation before planting yet another bee garden

"We've started holding our first community meetings, and we've organized a series of school strikes for climate change, in solidarity with Greta Thunberg. Hopefully, Two Degrees will be an even bigger success than the Bee City thing, but we'll see how that goes."

> **"Y**outh can't just stand aside. Because this is our future we're talking about. It's not something we get to give up on.**"**

REVOLUTION

Just before wrapping up Ethan's story, almost a year after we talked, I was curious about one loose end he'd mentioned near the end of our interview—applying to get his high school designated as a fully certified Bee School. He sounded typically hopeful but had mentioned some snags he'd run into. I wondered if the idea had fizzled, a bit like his Blue Dot proposal almost did way back in Grade 9. He was in Grade 12 now, probably too busy to be writing boring applications, anyway.

I go to the Bee City website and discover that, among Canada's thirty bee schools, there's one newly designated high school from Stratford, Ethan's home town. There's a picture of a male student tending a "pollinator garden and food forest." I zoom in on the photo.

Not Ethan. *Maybe he took the picture?*

I am invited to "Read their Application" and I instantly click on the link. This is surprising because I usually find reading somebody else's proposal or grant application or whatever as exciting as watching paint dry. But I knew that Ethan was pretty good at spinning those kinds of things and, wherever his passion flowed, the action usually followed. Final exams or no, I didn't think he'd let this baby go.

I open the Bee City School application form, the whole text of which is online, I suppose to inspire other schools to get on the bandwagon. I check the name of the school. Stratford Central Secondary School. *Yup, that's Ethan's all right.* I squint at the fine print below the official Bee City Canada logo—a stylized five-petaled flower, one petal of which is the striped butt of a bee. "Connecting People, Pollinators, and Places." Knowing Ethan as I do, I'm thinking, *Hmm, that definitely sounds like something he'd rally round.*

I realize I'm hunting for his hand in the application.

I scroll down through some initial blah blah, then stop at these words: ". . . a Bee School designation will help start a conversation about individual actions our students can take . . ."

Totally Ethan.

I lean into my screen, scrolling more slowly through the "Commitments and Actions" section. I learn that to get the official Bee School blessing, a school must agree to set up a "Bee City Working Group" made up of at least two teachers, two students, plus some kind of "caretaking staff"—maybe to look after the gardens when everyone else bags off for the summer?

The first student is an environmental changemaker named Ethan Elliott.

Yes!

Two more students are listed.

I guess they squeezed in an extra student.

I scroll to the next page.

Yet two more students, five in all. Only one teacher. No caretaker. That's it.

Obviously, a student-led bee revolution!

After a few more pages of "Requirements" and "Resolutions"—all promoting a better world for pollinators and people—the principal officially endorses the revolution with his hastily scribbled signature.

But there's more.

I have to smile at the application's bottom line. Final approval is granted not by the principal but by Ethan Elliott's signature, written in an unusually clear and careful hand.

> *"I have faith in the legions of activists rising up around the world. I have faith that we won't get to complete disaster. But if we don't rise up, if we don't take action now, there's always that possibility."*

TRAILBLAZER TIPS
....

Your voice matters

No matter what anybody says, your voice is super important. You can take on anything. I've seen how powerful that youth voice can be and how eager politicians are to engage with us.

Be an everyday activist

It's the daily commitment of individuals, lowering their resource use and rising up for change, that can make the biggest impact in this movement.

Caring counts

With a little bit of nudging, you can get someone to really care and take action. That means the world of difference. People don't get just how important caring is as a key step to action.

Tell a story

Tell a story about why you care about an issue. Keep it positive and personal. Don't dwell on the doom and gloom. Help people make a personal connection to the issue and they'll care more.

Start a conversation

Get people talking about issues in new and creative ways. Just helping one person understand the importance of an issue, and take action on it, can have a huge ripple effect on others.

Use online tools

Technology can encourage people to get more involved. It gives us an unprecedented ability to connect. I can't imagine trying to organize an environmental protest or event without it.

Act now

Don't wait to rise up and use your voice to make a change. Don't wait around for someone else to take action. Do it now. Our future relies upon the actions we do today.

"She was a trailblazer, the first Western researcher, man or woman, to study any animal in the wild in Africa."

– Anna Maria Tremonti, CBC

"[Anne's is a story of] one person's intellectual imagination, spirit of adventure, and daring: where she has long dreamed of going, where others either say she shouldn't or cannot go, and where some work against her going, she goes."

– Mark Behr, Writer

ANNE INNIS DAGG

The Woman Who Loves Giraffes
Pioneering wildlife research in Africa

Home: Waterloo, Ontario
Pursuits: "Giraffologist," citizen scientist, and writer

"Hi Jamie," Anne writes in an email before our interview in September 2018. "You may be interested in a film that has just been released about me called, The Woman Who Loves Giraffes. *It premiered last week in Calgary and Halifax, with standing ovations, and will be shown in Toronto this week. I think all the tickets are already sold out." She tells me she has just returned from several film festivals across Canada to discover 500 emails on her computer, mostly fan mail.*

As the world's First Lady of African wildlife research, studying giraffes long before Jane Goodall and her chimpanzees dazzled the world, Anne's fame and recognition are well deserved.

But it was not always so.

OBSESSION

It all started in a zoo. What Anne calls her "mania" for giraffes.

One summer day, back in 1936, when Anne was just a toddler, her mother took her on a train trip from their home in Toronto to Chicago to see Anne's grandparents. They visited the Brookfield Zoo. When they got to the giraffes, three-year-old Anne stopped dead in her tracks, eyes wide, to stare up and up at these unbelievable creatures.

➤ *Still beaming from her first encounter with a giraffe*

"I was entranced! I'm not sure what thrilled me most—their great height, their long neck and legs, their dark eyes. I only knew that I was smitten."

The giraffe instantly became her favorite animal.

Alas, there were no giraffes back at Toronto's Riverdale zoo, nor anywhere in Canada. So, Anne had to content herself with drawing pictures of them, showing giraffes engaged in all sorts of adventures. "When I was able to read, I hunted for books on them. To my disgust, I found there were none. So I thought, 'I'll learn all about giraffes and then *I'll* write one.'"

Anne filled the giraffe gap by reading about other animals like beaver, muskrat, and raccoons in books that her father gave her every Christmas.

Looking back over 85 years, Anne believes that her deep love of animals likely rubbed off from her father, Harold Innis. He grew up on a farm, milking cows, doing chores, trapping muskrats. "He was deeply interested in natural history and the behavior of wild animals. Every spring, he would listen for the first sound of crows, which meant, at last, the end of a long winter."

As a busy history professor teaching at the University of Toronto, he retained a fondness for wild things, even if found at the bottom of Anne's cereal bowl. "Once when he saw me painstakingly searching each raspberry in a dish to make sure there were no tiny worms on it, he rolled his eyes, grabbed a handful of berries, and ate them, worms and all."

Anne grew up during the Depression in a fine brick house near what then was the north edge of Toronto. The largest animals roaming around her neighborhood were horses, pulling wagons that delivered milk, bread, and ice door to door. "When chips of ice fell onto the road, we fought other kids to brush aside the horse manure and snatch them up to suck, enjoying the coldness."

Anne lived near a natural ravine where she and a gaggle of friends spent hours and hours playing in the woods. She always loved going to the cottage north of Toronto where her family spent whole summers until she was eleven. "Our glorious days were filled with swimming, exploring, games, and long walks—a child's paradise." On some of those walks, they came across a skunk or porcupine, and her father would taunt the animals while the rest of the family backed away. "He seemed to know exactly how far he could go without unpleasant circumstances."

➤ Anne (L) with Mary Williamson, fellow outdoor adventurer and lifelong friend

When Anne fell sick with scarlet fever at age eleven and had to be locked away in a hospital ward for one month, her mother made her three stuffed giraffes—a mother, father, and youngster. Anne clutched them tighter than ever when she learned that, because of possible germs, they would have to be destroyed when she left the hospital. Sensing Anne's anguish, a sympathetic nurse arranged to have her giraffe family "sterilized so they could live on" after Anne's release.

By the time Anne was in middle school, she was a confirmed bookaholic. "I loved books. And I loved everything about school. How wonderful to learn new things every single day! When I had to give a talk at school, my friends sat quietly while I expounded on the giraffe's long neck and spotted coat, holding up crayoned pictures I had made to captivate them. Thanks, *Book of Knowledge*. My family and friends were amused by this obsession."

Anne came by her love of learning naturally. "My father worked hard, both at the university and for long hours at home, reading or writing in his study." On Sunday afternoons, his students or colleagues would often pop in for lively discussions over tea and baked goodies. Even at a young age, Anne and her siblings liked to hang out in the hall, giggling at their conversation—until her father "thumbed his nose at us, without, he hoped, his guests noticing."

The bookish talk continued after the guests left, as did Anne's interest. "We always ate as a family round the dining room table, and I enjoyed listening to the talk of university affairs."

Anne's mother, Mary, also had a scholarly bent and wrote several books, including one requested by Anne's dad. Called *An Economic History of Canada*, it remains a key resource for economics students to this day. She later became dean of women at University College and continued writing almost to her dying day.

"I have been greatly influenced by my parents' academic interests and have spent my whole life reading, researching, and writing. From an early age, I made out a three-by-five-inch filing card for each book I read. I now have many thousands of such cards, which ensure I never read a book twice."

After Anne turned twelve, she started working part time at Toronto's Deer Park Library where, no surprise, she "read reams of books." She loved her library work and stayed on well into her teen years. Over the years, she watched her salary skyrocket from 25 cents to 43 cents an hour—"almost a miracle!" By the time she was eighteen, she had saved enough money to buy the $25 watch she had coveted for years and which later proved invaluable for her giraffe research.

While still working at the library, Anne founded her own newspaper, *The Giraffe Gazette*. The first issue contained two scholarly articles—one on the life of a toad, and the other on how to make a bow and arrow. As demanding as running a newspaper can be, with Anne taking on everything from writing and editing to printing and distribution, she successfully avoided burnout. There was no second issue.

Soon after Anne turned thirteen in 1946, she chose to attend the Bishop Strachan School, a private girls' school a block and a half from their new home in Toronto's Forest Hill district. "We were taught to be modest, frugal, and to always act like ladies. I adored every minute of my five years there. I loved sports, I loved my studies, I loved my family, and our dog, Tigger, and being outside to bicycle and read in the summers."

Anne was particularly enthralled with the line-up of sports offered at Bishop Strachan and was out every day after class, playing badminton, hockey, lacrosse, basketball or, her "game of choice," tennis, a sport she was crazy about—until she finally hung up her racquet in her 80s.

Like her parents, Anne had an itch for history. While studying ancient Greek and Roman cultures at school, she remembers swapping stories about this long-gone world with her father, while strolling around their park-like neighborhood. "I can still recall the thrill of those warm evenings, ambling under the leafy trees, soaking up everything he said, proud that he considered me a worthy listener."

Soon after these memorable walks, Anne lost her father to cancer. "Only later did I realize what an important scholar

➤ *"My father was deeply interested in natural history and the behavior of wild animals."*

my father had been, not only at the University of Toronto but far beyond. And perhaps how lucky I was to have somehow inherited his work ethic."

Throughout her high school years, Anne's giraffe obsession never let go, especially after a return visit to Chicago.

"When I was seventeen, my mother and I made another pilgrimage to the Brookfield Zoo, our first destination, of course, the giraffe house. The giraffe were magnificent. A lordly male leaned over the fence and stared down at me with huge brown eyes. I gazed with reverence back at him. My passion for giraffe was firmer than ever."

Anne set her sights on studying zoology—and the giraffe—the day she entered high school. She learned she would have to plow through four years of other courses before zoology was offered but, when she finally got to Grade 13, she hit a wall. "In my final year, I found that if I wanted to enrol in Honors Science at university, I had to take chemistry and physics instead of zoology. Zoology had to wait yet another year!"

Second visit to the Chicago Zoo at age 17:
"My passion for giraffe was firmer than ever."

When Anne arrived at the University of Toronto in 1951, the giraffe remained her first love. "Of course, I enrolled in biology. My goal was to earn my degree, then spend a year in Africa studying giraffe."

She describes her first-year course load as "horrendous."

"I struggled with English, French, geology, physics, chemistry (eight hours a week), mathematics, and botany." And *finally* zoology! But the long-awaited course did not pan out as she'd hoped. The class started by concentrating on the amoeba, and progressed painstakingly via worms and frogs to rabbits. Surely they would move on to larger mammals like the giraffe, Anne thought. But no. She was forced to memorize the names of countless clams, fish, and bugs. "We learned nothing about giraffes."

Any scientific articles on giraffes that Anne rooted out on her own mostly dealt with the anatomy of dead animals, the naming of different races, or guesswork on how such a strange animal evolved. She learned zero about the living, breathing wonder that haunted her dreams.

Anne's mother had predicted that her university days would be the happiest days of her life. Anne wasn't too sure about that, especially when assaulted by so many courses. *Surely greater times would come later on,* she thought. But eventually she agreed with her mother. "To be free for four years to learn what you want to know and to have good friends learning along with you was indeed magnificent."

Sports remained Anne's go-to for blowing off steam. She was constantly on the lookout for tennis buddies and squeezed in games whenever she could. She joined the university woman's hockey team but, as much fun as they had, they never tasted the thrill of victory. "We must have been the worst team on record because we never scored a goal in four years of play."

Throughout the agony and ecstasy of university life, Anne kept fanning the flames of her African dream—which usually triggered skepticism or outright laughter. "Back then, if I did mention my ambition to study giraffe in Africa to faculty members or anyone else, they laughed heartily at its absurdity."

So what if Anne happened to be the first zoologist—male or female—to go to Africa to do a long-term wildlife study? Little did she care that she might be blazing a research trail to be followed, years later, by such famous field scientists as Jane Goodall studying chimpanzees in the jungles of Tanganyika, or Dian Fossey studying gorillas in the mountains of Rwanda. All Anne really wanted to do was go study her beloved giraffe in the wild and learn how they interact, how they move, what they eat—basically, how they *live*.

Trouble is, the science of animal behavior, or ethology, had not been invented in 1955 when Anne started gearing up to go to Africa. Any professors who took her plan seriously— of which there were few—had no clue how to do such work. They confessed to Anne that they knew no one who had actually studied the behavior of *any* animal on its home turf. Okay, what about books on animal behavior? Her professors

Chatting with a friendly racoon in the University of Toronto's Zoology lab

could only shrug. All Anne managed to find was a dusty old study of red deer in the highlands of Scotland.

Undeterred by laughter or the lack of research, Anne soldiered on, looking for ways to save money for her Africa trip. In the summers, she "worked as a gofer" at a medical lab and cleaned gunk off mammal skulls at the Royal Ontario Museum. Working in the lab opened her eyes to the cruelty that mice, rats, and monkeys were subjected to. In one case, she witnessed a researcher sewing a large glass bulb into the stomach of a living mouse "just to see how it went." Years later she would publish articles citing other examples of research cruelty and lobbied for more humane laboratory protocols.

During her final years as an undergrad student, she snagged a lucrative job as a lab instructor—teaching younger students the names of clams and fish and bugs. On her graduation day, she was able to top up her African nest egg with a $500 gold medal biology award—a good chunk of change in those days.

"Thanks to my savings, my gold medal money, and the kindness of my worried mother, I now had $2,000, which I trusted would last me a year in Africa."

The money was in the bag. It was time to organize the trip of a lifetime.

Her big question off the top was: Where to go?

Anne wanted to live somewhere near wild giraffes so she could observe them day after day, month after month. She fired letters off to wildlife departments and universities in every African country where giraffes lived. All responses were universally polite and unhelpful. Several letters implied that a lone white woman from Canada might have problems pulling off this kind of stunt.

After that, she began to sign her query letters as "A. Innis," implying that maybe she was a man.

By the summer of 1955 she still had no African leads in sight. "Not knowing what else to do, I enrolled for a master's degree in genetics, a subject I adored. In my genetics class in 1953, our euphoric professor strode into the classroom one day to announce that the structure of DNA had just been discovered. How amazing is that?"

Her own research was "much less exalted," studying the genetics of different strains of mice. "My friends had a wonderful time joking about research on mice as a prelude to studying giraffe."

Anne's breakthrough came near the end of her Masters' program with the random arrival of a fellow graduate student, Rufus Churcher, from, of all places, Rhodes University in Grahamstown, South Africa. He knew someone there who had been introduced to a park giraffe named Shorty, transplanted from a wild herd on a ranch far to the north. Apparently, the ranch owner, Alexander Matthew, was protecting almost a hundred giraffes on his property and might welcome someone to study them.

"I was euphoric!"

Anne wrote to the rancher immediately, again signing A. Innis. "To be on the safe side, I didn't mention that I was a girl." Mr. Matthew promptly wrote back with a friendly invitation to come study his giraffes and bunk down with his cowhands.

"But he obviously thinks you're a man!" said Anne's mother when she heard the news.

"Well, I can sort that out later," Anne told her.

She had to run and buy a boat ticket to England.

AFRICA BOUND
∙∙∙∙∙∙∙∙∙∙∙∙∙∙∙∙∙∙∙∙∙∙

Anne's mother waved goodbye at Toronto's Union Station as her intrepid daughter boarded an eastbound train to catch an ocean liner. Anne traveled light, wearing a small knapsack and carrying a suitcase packed with just three skirts and three blouses. Soon after getting to London, she visited a secondhand bookstore and filled the rest of her suitcase with eight weighty books on the history, cultures, and landscapes of Africa. "Next to the giraffe, I was anxious to learn about the continent that I'd dreamed about for so many years."

While in London, she also took time to write Mr. Matthew again, telling him how thrilled she was to be on her way to his ranch. This time she stuck her neck out and signed as a woman.

From England, Anne sailed south for two weeks on a ship bound for South Africa. She spent much of this trip leaning over the deck rail, watching leaping porpoises, flying fish, soaring albatross, or, at night, luminous plankton that ignited in time with each turn of the ship's propeller. She also amused herself talking with a group of British botanists, playing party games with a team of twenty Welsh rugby players, and diving deep into her Africa books.

Anne was warmly welcomed into the Rhodes University family of zoologists. But she was surprised to learn that, even here, there was very little known scientifically about African animals. One professor she befriended admitted to collecting road-kills from the ditch to learn more about local wildlife. Another professor joked that, "Things must be really bad if we need a girl from Canada to come and study our African fauna!"

Anne takes Camelo for a test drive before her multi-day excursion through the "boonies" of South Africa.

She got another surprise when she learned that the ranch where she hoped to study giraffes was over a thousand miles away and was inaccessible by plane, train, or bus. Her new friends told her she would have to buy a car and drive herself.

Unfazed by the prospect of a multi-day drive through the "boonies" of South Africa on iffy roads full of strangers and, possibly, deadly snakes, Anne pressed on. She scoured the local used car ads and bought a Ford Prefect for $200. She didn't care that its top speed was only fifty miles an hour and that it might need water in the radiator every twenty minutes. It was her first car and she was thrilled, even giving it a name—Camelo—short for the giraffe's scientific name, *Camelopardalis*.

So, Anne was all set to go, right?

Wrong.

Anne's biggest surprise came a few days after buying Camelo: a letter from Mr. Matthew calling the whole thing off. With his wife and daughter away, he had a problem with the optics. "It wouldn't be proper for you to live in my house without a chaperone," he wrote.

Feeling "baffled and distraught," Anne wrote an impassioned plea back to Mr. Matthew. His response came by telegram after a long, nail-biting week.

"I could come after all, since I was so keen."

Anne set off at dawn the next day and drove till dusk. She did the same the next day, driving full throttle until the last eighty miles, which were "miserable." Anne slowly picked her way over endless stretches of unpaved washboard roads. Camelo shuddered and shook until she could take it no more and stopped dead in a cloud of steam a few miles from Matthew's ranch.

"By this time, it was ten o'clock on a moonless night. Once I turned off the car's headlights, the darkness was total. There was nothing but silence. I was terrified. I had seen no buildings or other cars for over an hour. This was truly the domain of lions and leopards, drunken men, and adders—I had seen several of these snakes squashed on the road earlier in the day."

She tried locking herself in the car until daylight but just worked herself into a frenzy. She popped out of Camelo and started inching her way forward in the dark. "My heart pounded in terror for almost an hour until finally a car approached and I flagged it down."

"You must be the Canadian girl," said the guy at the wheel, who turned out to be Matthew's right-hand man.

"With these words I knew I was safe."

IN THE FIELD
·····················

Right away, Anne discovered Mr. Matthew to be "very kind and hospitable." He let her take over his daughter's room in the ranch house and insisted that she use his state-of-the-art 16-millimeter movie camera (remember, it's 1956) and his powerful binoculars for her giraffe work.

The first morning, he took Anne on a private tour of his farm, past rows of grapefruit and lemon trees, past sprawling cattle pastures, until they got to a waterhole that he knew was a magnet for giraffes.

➤ *Rancher Alexander Matthew and one of nearly 100 wild giraffes on his farm*

There!

Anne's first wild giraffe, a female, accompanied by four impala, coming in for a drink. "She's gorgeous and she's huge!" whispers Anne, guessing she could walk upright under the giraffe's belly. She and Mr. Matthew watch the giraffe bend her legs and swoop her head down for a long drink, then yank it back up again to her full, impossible height. Already the scientist in Anne is asking questions. "I wondered, why doesn't she faint from the rapid change in blood pressure in her brain?"

The next morning Anne set off alone in Camelo to launch her giraffe work. She encountered a male giraffe, so huge and so close that, through binoculars, she could only examine parts of his body at a time—an amazingly long leg, the tattoo-like torso, the impossible neck, the magnificent head. Driving past a forested section of road, she had to laugh when she

Early in her fieldwork, Anne once mistook giraffe legs for trees until the animals stepped out onto the road.

Every five minutes, Anne recorded the behavior of each giraffe in sight.

realized that what she thought were trees were actually the legs of five more giraffe! She visited another waterhole and spotted a male and female some distance away. Anne got out of Camelo and walked slowly toward them, thrilled. The male galloped over to the female—and they bolted.

Lesson learned. Stay in the car.

And so Anne's scientific adventure began.

It didn't take long for her to slip into a routine of field research like she'd been preparing for it all her life, which, in a way, she had.

She selected and mapped the best giraffe viewing areas. She could soon identify individual animals and named them according to prominent features, like Star, a male with pointy body spots, and Pom-pom, a female with extra hairy horns.

Every five minutes, Anne recorded in her field book the specific behavior of each giraffe in sight—standing, lying down, pacing, pawing, cud chewing, neck banging, sparring, sleeping, suckling young. She wrote "browsing" more than any other activity because giraffes, she learned, mostly keep busy eating their daily quota of leaves, often seventy or eighty pounds a day. Rarely, she wrote "mounting" as she witnessed reproductive behavior among giraffes never before recorded by science, including occasional steamy love scenes between two males.

Anne learned to sweat it out inside her car, recording observations, to lower the risk of giraffes galloping away any time she popped out.

Anne recorded all her observations while sitting in her stifling hot car.

Except the one time she didn't.

"I exited Camelo to do ballet exercises beside her, using her handle as a *barre*. It was incredibly hot and cramped sitting inside the tiny car, waiting for each five-minute interval to be up." That's when Anne noticed a giraffe making a beeline toward her, trying to figure out what was up. She knew she'd influenced the animal's natural activities, a big no-no in behavioral science. "Sadly, I slipped back into Camelo to spend more hours sweating over my clipboard."

But the sweat paid off.

Hundreds of hours sitting in her sweltering car gave Anne a pile of notebooks crammed with careful observations. Before leaving Africa almost a year later, she organized her notes into one "interesting and insightful document." This, plus the hours of unique movie footage she'd captured, built the foundation for "reams" of scientific publications and scientific film clips down the road.

Near the end of her year, Anne took time off to tour some of South Africa's best wildlife parks and to climb Mount Kilimanjaro in Tanzania. A week before leaving, Matthew gave her a Zulu shield made from the hide of a young giraffe killed by a lion. On the back of the shield were the words, "*Inkosikas-ka-Uhlu*," Zulu for "Laughing Lady," Anne's nickname among the ranch workers. Matthew also gave her a beautiful wool blanket adorned with giraffe figures that continues to keep her warm, "both physically and spiritually," over sixty years later.

➤ Anne is with her traveling companion, Fernandez, after climbing Mount Kilimanjaro, Africa's highest mountain. "It was a kind of hell," she admits, but the smiles say it was worth it.

"It felt wonderful to have had a dream and been able to accomplish it," says Anne, reflecting on her glorious time in Africa.

Her next big dream—to become a full-fledged professor—did not go nearly so well.

Anne stands by a giraffe mysteriously shot by a local warden. Always the scientist, she did a dissection before the meat was distributed among local farm workers.

PROFESSOR BLUES
....

The wheels of Anne's scientific mind got spinning again soon after returning to Canada. Having married Ian Dagg, a former tennis buddy from her U. of T. days, she had settled in Waterloo, Ontario, another university town where Ian taught physics. Before leaving Africa, Anne had sent several hefty bags of dried leaves, favored by giraffe, plus samples of their marble-shaped feces to her "long-suffering" mother in Toronto. Anne was curious about the chemistry of giraffe nutrition and recruited Waterloo's chemistry department to analyze her precious shipment. The leaf studies led to one of Anne's many scientific reports. "As for the feces, they proved to be far more enigmatic than the leaves. I buried them in the back yard when no one was looking."

In reviewing the rolls and rolls of giraffe footage she'd shot at Matthew's ranch, Anne became eager to learn exactly how this unlikely creature moved in comparison to other large mammals. Perhaps a PhD topic some day?

While starting a family, Anne chose to pursue her research independently and still made time to teach one biology course at Waterloo Lutheran University (now Wilfred Laurier).

There were times when she felt the world had taken her ground-breaking research seriously, like the American television network that paid her handsomely for her film footage of a rowdy fight between two male giraffes. Or when the American Society of Mammalogists invited her to Illinois to speak at their annual meeting. "I felt like a true scientist for the first time, although the master of ceremonies, when introducing me, got all three of my names wrong, calling me

'Miss Annie Dog.' Despite this, scores of men in suits listened intently to my talk."

The first hint that Anne's career hopes might be derailed by sexism hit when she asked the university if she could teach another course. They basically told her that two courses a year was fine for men, but not for her.

That settled it. Time for Anne to get that PhD.

Which she did, after several crazy busy years.

"I was not only taking the required courses of the degree and researching and writing my thesis, but also looking after three young children, making all the meals for the family, and doing all the housework."

Ten years after returning from Africa, Anne added the letters "PhD" to her name. "I now hoped to become a tenured professor like my father, my husband, and my brother. Why not?"

She had all the trimmings to get tenure. She'd done this amazing research. Had tons of publications to her name. A great teaching record.

Why not?

Well, the University of Waterloo's Dean of Science told her why not. He simply did not hire women, no matter how talented. He felt their place was in the home, serving the family. Besides, Anne had a professor husband so obviously didn't need the money, right?

Anne and five other women with biology PhD's didn't even get job interviews.

"I was devastated."

Though she eventually found a good teaching job at the University of Guelph, they, too, denied her full professorship for similar reasons. Waterloo Lutheran University (WLU) also turned her down in favor of a man "with far fewer recommendations than I had," Anne says.

The WLU decision was the last straw for Anne. She filed a complaint with the Ontario Human Rights Commission to dispute the decision. This was in the mid-1970s when the women's liberation movement was making waves around the world. But, after a heated seven-year battle, she lost the case and was forced to mothball her dreams for future giraffe research.

VINDICATION

After slamming into so many closed academic doors just because of her gender, did Anne retreat to the suburbs of Waterloo to live out a life of domestic servitude?

Hardly.

Instead, she redefined herself as an independent "citizen scientist." In this new role, Anne enjoyed the freedom to throw herself into her own research and writing projects, always guided by strict scientific standards but unshackled by anyone else's baggage or agenda—including universities, governments, or corporations.

"To be happy, I have to be working on some goal. For a time, when I was a teenager, this goal was to be the best in tennis. As an adult, it has been to accomplish some project or to finish an article or a book I am writing."

Anne admits there is a downside to this unique path. "Citizen scientists frequently work alone, using their own money to carry out their projects."

But when such scientists find each other and team up, magic can happen. So Anne discovered when she met Hilde Pilters, a PhD-trained biologist from Germany who was doing independent studies of camel behavior in the Saharan Desert. They became good friends and, for two adventurous summers, Anne joined Hilde in Mauritania, in Saharan Africa, riding camels over giant sand dunes, and later publishing an award-winning book together on the behavior, ecology, and importance of camels.

Anne describes her work life over the five decades since earning her PhD as "similar to the feat of a long-distance runner"—sharing her path with kindred scientists, working on a joint project for a while, then going their separate ways. "This has resulted in many friendships and a number of very

Studying camel behavior on a research trip in the Saharan Desert

satisfying multi-authored enterprises. Co-authoring an article or book is paradise."

Anne's writing covers an amazing "potpourri of interests," including: the mating habits of giraffe, homosexual behavior in large mammals, Australia's controversial kangaroo hunt, climbing Mount Kilimanjaro, sexism and discrimination in academia, plus a fun kids' book she'd promised to write long ago called 5 *Giraffes*.

In her 2016 autobiography, *Smitten by Giraffe*, I count over 80 publications with her name on them. The one that really jumps out for me is her 1976 title, *The Giraffe: Its Biology, Behavior, and Ecology*. This one-of-a-kind book remains the bible for giraffe keepers around the world—like Amy Phelps who looks after giraffes at the San Francisco Zoo.

"When I was in high school, I knew I wanted to be a giraffe keeper," says Amy in a recent CBC radio show about Anne. "I loved Anne and I read her book first. It was really hard to go through at fifteen, but I did it. I highlighted it. I took notes and I memorized every little piece of giraffe information. I worked in the field for over ten years and most of what we relied on, still, was Anne's book from so long ago."

In 2010, Amy tracked Anne down and invited her to an international conference of giraffe workers, where she was presented with the first ever Anne Dagg Pioneer Award for giraffe research.

For Anne, being celebrated by a community of giraffe experts "was just amazing." She regrets that she did not get to work with those young scientists throughout her career. "I wish I had known them, but I know a lot of them now, and that's wonderful!"

Anne's rediscovery as a world-renowned "giraffologist" inspired movie director Alison Reid to make a film about her—*The Woman Who Loves Giraffes*. What inspired her was Anne's adventurous and tenacious spirit. "She wasn't fazed at all by what obstacles were in her way. She just always found the 'yes.'"

Released in the fall of 2018, this hugely popular film blew the lid off Anne's public profile, resulting in media splashes across the country and beyond. The story of this largely unknown wildlife pioneer, overshadowed by the likes of Jane Goodall, and mocked or ignored by narrow-minded professors, leapt off the movie screen onto the radar of animal lovers and biologists around the world.

Among the thousands that picked up Anne's story was an official government committee responsible for identifying "outstanding Canadians whose lifelong contributions have made the world a better place." The committee reviewed Anne's file, watched her film, and gave her thumbs up all around. In December 2019, they unveiled Anne's name on a list of stellar Canadians who had earned one of the country's highest kudos, an Order of Canada award.

"I hope we can get more women and girls interested in this sort of thing," Anne told a journalist upon receiving her award. "It's just so exciting to find that people are now amazed that I've done all that!"

TRAILBLAZER TIPS
· ·

Get out in the field
Many children do not have the chance to go into the wild. Encourage your school to organize excursions to natural areas to experience wildlife and undisturbed nature.

Keep an eye on urban green spaces
Parks and forests in or near towns where children can see different plants and animals are often the most threatened. Do all you can to protect and publicize the value of these precious areas.

Join a group
I fear that by the middle of the century, many large mammals may be killed off entirely. If you want to make a difference to wildlife and nature, join a local or national conservation group.

Build a resource pool
Find knowledgeable and youth-friendly resource people to talk to students at school, or take them into the field to check out various environments and their species.

Do a photo contest
Organize a contest for students to take photos in different categories, such as: wild animals, habitats, plants, or problems (e.g., pollution, habitat destruction). Include a school slideshow, prizes, and other fun activities.

Hunt for young heroes

Many young people are doing wonderful environmental work.
Find them and bring them to your school for an inspiring talk,
walk, or workshop.

"Kathleen Martin is a tiger, not a turtle."

– Peter Carver, Editor

KATHLEEN MARTIN

· ·

Sea Turtle Sentinel

Finding beauty, justice, and joy
in rescuing a dinosaur

Home: Halifax, Nova Scotia
Pursuits: Sea turtle activist, author, educator

I can't remember when I last talked with Kathleen Martin. "We worked together on your book tour a lifetime ago," she reminds me after I finally track her down. When she's not working as Executive Director of the Canadian Sea Turtle Network—which is basically 24/7—she keeps a toe in the local writing community, occasionally shepherding visiting authors like me. Though I'd never been to Halifax before that tour, she made me feel instantly at home. Another thing she'll steal time for is family camping trips to Kejimkujik National Park, in the wild western heart of Nova Scotia. She'd just returned from there when we talked. Between the usual wandering down trails, gazing at stars, or just sitting by a lake, Kathleen had

*to respond to yet another emergency on her sea turtle hotline.
"This happens almost every year!" she tells me. It all goes with
a job she never expected and dearly loves.*

SURFACING

The leatherback turtle's eyes looked old the day she hatched
seventy years ago, with their heavy wrinkled lids and intense
stare. She blinks in the sunlight as her rocket-shaped head
emerges from the sea. She inhales deeply, letting her gigantic
teardrop-shaped body roll in the waves. A stubby antenna
pivots over her broad black back, beaming signals to a satellite
orbiting thousands of kilometers above the Earth.

Her lungs now brimming with an hour's-worth of air, the
turtle flaps her wing-like front flippers, a shape perfected a
hundred million years ago, and drops below the waves. Pink
tentacles trail like jewelry from her thick neck, remnants of her
latest meal—a lion's mane jellyfish. She flies swiftly, effortlessly,
spiraling down and down through the sun-streaked surface
waters, then disappears into the midnight depths.

*"Sometimes I am struck silent by the weightlessness of
words,"* writes Kathleen, in her well-read blog about
sea turtles. *"They tumble and break around us and still
I can't make them loud enough to show what the ocean
is. The pleasant crackling of corophium in the mud . . ."*

Kathleen is challenging us here, wants us to ask ourselves,
"What's *that*?" To Google it, or maybe go ask a fisherman. She

A giant leatherback turtle crawls back to the sea after laying over 100 eggs on a protected beach in the U.S. Virgin Islands.

wants us to connect with a place she loves, where she might have rescued a stranded sea turtle that just washed in from as far away as Trinidad, Colombia, or French Guiana. She wants us to feel that place. To hear it. To make it real. That's the way she writes. She's calling us to stop, look, and listen. Corophium? They're a skinny, sand-burrowing crustacean that you'll probably never see. But if you've ever set foot on a healthy seaside beach in Nova Scotia, you've heard their snappy applause.

But, back to Kathleen's blog.

> *". . . The shifting smell of saltwater, laced sometimes with dried seaweed, sometimes with whipping wind. The quality of the grayish turquoise of the back of a blue whale as it arcs endlessly just in front of a boat.*
> *So I have told myself that you know already why it matters that we have sea turtles in the world . . ."*

Funny thing is, this didn't always matter to Kathleen. Our planet's aching need for sea turtles.

STUDENT OF BEAUTY
····································

Kathleen has not always looked to the sea to find beauty and purpose and love.

"You've been around," I say as Kathleen and I settle into an afternoon-long conversation. "You're born in the urban jungle of Toronto, you move to the Canadian Shield of Sudbury, to the cornfields of Spring Valley, Illinois, and end up on the seacoast of Halifax."

"I was only an infant in Toronto, so that doesn't register on my consciousness as a childhood home. But Sudbury, absolutely. Back then it was still quite a wild place. We spent endless hours roaming the woods across from my house, picking blueberries, swimming in the city's many, many lakes.

➤ A child of Sudbury's Canadian Shield landscape

"We were out there, just kids, building tree forts with real tools. It was all basically unsupervised. Today's parents would think such activities were highly dangerous. Years later, I asked my mom about this. 'Oh, you were fine!' she said.

"We had a beaver pond hidden in the woods across the street. In winter, we would tramp to it, breaking through the new snow with our boots. My older brother, Jimmy, and his friends would shovel off a big rectangle of the pond for them to play hockey, and over a little further, a little rink for my friends and me. It was beautiful thick black ice and we loved it. We were surrounded by hills of rock, which made everything feel private and safe. Our own world.

"So I really feel connected to the Canadian Shield, to that particular type of rock and the lichens, the birch trees, all those lakes. We'd go biking and swim off the beaches all summer long. I have a really deep love of lakes. You know, the way you feel when you're smelling lake water while swimming in it. That's very different from the ocean. Even now, as I've studied the ocean, spent lots of time on it, and certainly have a deep love for it, there is *nothing* that gets me like swimming in a northern Ontario lake.

"I wasn't the kid who was out exploring nature in a specific way. I wasn't studying it or turning over rocks, looking for salamanders, or trying to catch snakes. But because of where we lived, I was always in nature. I spent a lot of time around trees. I'd stay up in my favorite tree, reading a book or writing."

"That's a beautiful image, Kathleen."

"I loved creating stories. Even then, I very much wanted to be a writer. Because truly, in my core, that is what I am."

"Can you take me back to your headspace up in the trees, reading, creating?"

Kathleen laughs. "That truly was my natural habitat! I had birches in my backyard and would climb up with my butcher paper—that red, crinkly paper you wrap meat in. I liked to write on it. I had pencils up there and a little space where I'd store my butcher paper. I'd climb up and sit and think and write."

"What would you write about?"

"Anything. Stories. Poems. What I was thinking or noticing. Like any writer, you get better and better if you can write about anything."

➤ Oct 10/84
"The moon is out tonight after being absent for a month. At least I couldn't see it. It looks like a pearl nestled in blue velvet, with rays shining North, South, East, and West. It's beautiful . . ."

"Sudbury must have been an awesome place to grow up."

"All that natural beauty. It became part of my magical childhood world, that sacred space you can only create with your childhood friends. We'd go outside and tell each other stories. Or I'd make them act out the books I was reading. 'We're doing *Little Women* today,' I'd say, 'and here are the characters. You are so-and-so. I'm obviously Jo. You're Beth and you're going to die. You're Amy and you get to wear a wedding dress.' We built playhouses and I'd stick them all in rooms. Luckily, I had friends with big imaginations."

"Was this a gaggle of girls or kind of a neighborhood scene?"

➤ *Since childhood, Kathleen has felt "a really deep love of lakes."*

"There were three girls I used to play with on the street all the time. But there were always boys around us. It was a very mixed group. The street was great. When it got dark, we'd play 'Old Ghost in the Graveyard' or 'Hide and Seek' and run through the woods. Lots of fun. The boys would wreck our tree house. Then we'd try to wreck theirs. The usual playful stuff."

"What about your parents? Were they big on the outdoors?"

"We never went camping as kids. We'd never do that. We were very much a hotel family. When we went somewhere, it was all about comfort and convenience."

"So, was it more like glamping—luxury camping?"

"No. There was none of the pain part. No camping words could describe anything my family did on vacation. We had nothing against the environment. My parents encouraged us to get outside. They loved to go on walks. My dad liked to fish, so sometimes we would hike out to a lake deep in the woods and go fishing. But only day trips. Nothing that involved sleeping in a tent. We'd go for cable TV and room service instead."

"So, where *did* Kathleen the environmentalist come from?"

"That wasn't something I was born with. I never came to nature as a young scientist or environmentalist. I didn't have any of that as a kid. My thing was just to be outside in the places I loved. And to be . . . it sounds a little strange . . . but to be a student of the *beauty* of nature. That's what I was doing outdoors, trying to understand it at the level of beauty that stops you in your tracks. My experience growing up with nature was more of an aesthetic one than scientific.

➤ *Kathleen in her teens enjoys a pensive moment boating on a Sudbury lake.*

"So, I wasn't the kid wanting to save the whales or dolphins or sea turtles. That just wasn't me. If you'd asked me if I wanted to save them, I'd say, of course. I'd always had a pervasive sense of justice, which I still hold."

"How did that take root, your sense of justice, of what's right and good?"

"We may never have gone camping when I was growing

up. And my parents may not have taught me about the natural world. But, boy, they *absolutely* gave me the training to stand up for what you believe in. That was one hundred percent the doctrine in my home. You stand up for people who need a voice, who need your help. It doesn't matter if you don't like what I'm saying, as long as it's true for me. I'm not trying to be rude. I always try to be polite about it. But I will absolutely say what I think. *That's* your job in the world."

"Your parents instilled this in you?"

"For sure. As an American, my father was a conscientious objector to the Vietnam war. My parents came of age in the 60s, protesting the war, standing up for what they believed in. They knew that their young voices mattered, that they had power, that they could speak truth to others who held power, that they could disagree with authorities. Invariably, when you looked at our grocery list on the wall, my dad would have written: 'World peace.' Or if a waitress asked at the end of a meal, 'Would you like anything else?' he would always say, 'World peace.' He was teasing but he wasn't joking. It was the thing that drove him. So, it was clear to me from a young age that there was a lot wrong with the world."

"And your mother?"

"My mom is a teacher. I remember when I was small, longing for her to stay home like my friends' moms. But she loved what she did and she was superb at it. And it wasn't long before I saw how wonderful it was that I had a mom who was working—not just to help her students, but in other ways, too. She helped in the fight to gain and protect equal rights for women teachers in Ontario. My mom also had a cousin, Father Abraham, who ran a project in northern India to help people in deep poverty. My parents visited there many times.

It taught me the importance of trying to help solve difficult problems in other parts of the world, too.

"My paternal grandmother was a lawyer way back when very few women went to university at all, let alone law school. She became the first female State Attorney in Illinois. There is a story about her refusing to bake something for a church fair until all the men lawyers did the same. It's a great example of how small everyday changes are the building blocks of broader social change."

"So, lots of people in your family standing up for what's right."

"I heard more about this from them as I got older. That reality gave our household a pervading sense that you stand up for what's right and what you say matters. I never, ever felt that my voice didn't have power,  which I think was quite a gift—it's an important gift to give to all young people. I was very lucky to grow up in a setting where that was the case."

> "*T*here are two things that matter most in environmental work.
> 1. **Justice.** Stand up for what's right and what's just. This applies to the environmental world as much as the human world.
> 2. **Beauty.** This world has so much beauty in it. Keep moving toward beauty if you want to stop all the myriad ways we hurt one another and the planet."

THE QUESTION

Now Kathleen thinks about environmental issues every day, and many nights. That's become second nature for her, whether on the job or not.

What does she think about?

Sea turtles, mostly leatherbacks, the oldest, biggest, widest-ranging, deepest-diving turtles on planet Earth. Hatched by the zillions on sandy beaches way down in Central and South America, only one in a thousand leatherbacks might grow to maturity and head north for the all-you-can-eat jellyfish buffet off the coast of Kathleen's adopted Nova Scotia home. A few hundred of them make it each year. A lot of them don't, drowned in fishing nets, choked by plastic bags, struck by ships, slaughtered for meat, or harvested for eggs. And if human stuff doesn't take them out, a shark just might.

Kathleen's job is to keep tabs on this critically endangered species, protect them, and celebrate them through a Halifax-based outfit that she co-founded and directs—the Canadian Sea Turtle Network (www.seaturtle.ca).

It all started when Kathleen fell in love with someone who had camped all his life.

Unlike his bride-to-be, Mike James was born a scientist. His love of sea turtles carried him through a ground-breaking PhD study that officially added leatherback turtles to the species map of Canada after decades of scientific skepticism. That love eventually rubbed off on Kathleen and—when they're not hungry—their kids.

"What I find interesting is why I decided to do this as a profession. My story may speak to people who aren't typically interested in environmental work. Initially I was very interested in journalism. I wasn't at all an environmentalist. When I went to university, I studied *nothing* in the sciences. No biology, no psychology. It was all English literature. I just wanted to read books and talk about books.

"But my husband, Mike, was absolutely passionate about the natural world. He started his graduate work on the conservation of sea turtles, eventually settling on leatherbacks. Canadians didn't know much about them, but there were several of them washing up dead on Nova Scotia beaches each year. So, I encouraged him to look at this brand-new thing.

"I remember talking to him several months into his PhD research, frustrated by how it was very quickly consuming our lives. I said, 'Well, these turtles really don't help us in any way. What's the difference if they go extinct? We don't get anything from them. Really, what are we losing here? Isn't this just evolution, a matter of survival of the fittest? Species that survive are meant to survive. Do we really need to interfere with this natural process and try to conserve them?'

"Mike just stopped and looked at me. He said, 'Kath, the whole world would lose so much without leatherbacks. It's not about what works for humans. It's not about us.' He explained that it's not evolution when all these threats, like fishing nets, happen so quickly. Human impacts are being imposed so fast, there's no time for turtles to adapt and evolve, especially when they're dying in such great numbers.

"I recall that conversation so clearly. And I thought, 'Oh, you're so right. This world isn't just about us. It belongs to *all* creatures as much as us. It's about how all of nature fits together. We're just a small part of this world, yet we have such an outsized impact.' I just wasn't educated about how

*Kathleen's husband, biologist Mike James, a global expert
on endangered leatherback sea turtles*

enormous and how fast human impacts really were. And how
unjust it all was."

"So this was an epiphany moment for you?" I ask. "A real
awakening?"

"Yes. Mike's answer forever changed me. It totally shifted
my perspective, and I knew at once that I could never shift
back. That's when it clicked that all those things I'd learned
at home or through studying literature or my parents' work
in the developing world—I'd seen how injustice works on a
human scale and always been passionate about countering it.
But that 'click' made me go, *Oh! It's the same with the natural
world!* And it's the same questions: Who gets control? Who
gets how much? Whose voice is loudest at the table? Well, the
reality is that nature has *no* voice, so as environmentalists, we
naturally become storytellers. We become the voice for the
voiceless.

"So that's why I became a true environmentalist."

PICKING UP THE TRAIL
··

Kathleen describes the Canadian Sea Turtle Network, which she skippers, as an offspring of her husband's PhD work. In the late 90s, Mike picked up a faint research trail abandoned decades earlier by Dr. Sherman Bleakney, the first Canadian biologist to shine the light of science on leatherback turtles.

➤ *Kathleen considers Dr. Sherman Bleakney a true hero, the first biologist to put leatherbacks on the species map of Canada.*

National Geographic writer, Tim Apenzeller, tells Bleakney's story in his 2009 article about leatherbacks, which he calls "ancient mariners." One August day in 1961, Bleakney got a phone call from a local fisherman about a strange sea creature he'd just unloaded on a Halifax wharf. When Bleakney showed up, he found a curious crowd circled around a giant black sea turtle that tipped the scales at 900 pounds. He immediately recognized it as a leatherback, renowned for its rubbery, streamlined shell and immense size.

But hang on. This was supposedly a tropical species.

To Bleakney, this dinosaur-like turtle, that had nested on

faraway beaches since before *T. rex* ruled the world, seemed as out of place in the ice-cold waters off Nova Scotia as "parrots in a Halifax park." But when he started asking around, he learned from local fishermen that they spotted leatherbacks so regularly at that time of year, they called it "turtle season."

As Bleakney gathered a pile of eyewitness reports from fishermen, he came to the "mind-boggling" conclusion that leatherbacks were surviving, even thriving, in water temperatures that would kill any other sea turtle. And they'd obviously come a long way. One dead turtle he examined had a tropical mangrove twig stuck in its eye. Warm-water barnacles had hitched a ride on the back of another. Even weirder, he discovered that their stomachs were stuffed with chewed-up jellyfish.

Clearly it was time for some serious research to figure out what the heck was going on with these giant turtles.

But few in the scientific community believed him.

Local fishermen told Bleakney that they spotted leatherbacks so often in late summer they called it "turtle season."

"People laughed at him," says Kathleen, who considers Bleakney a true hero. "They refused to fund him. They said, 'That's ridiculous, there's no way sea turtles are in cold Canadian waters.' And, you know, he had to shelve his work because no one gave him any research money. He went on to become a specialist in sea slugs. I remember him saying, 'Kathleen, you think it's hard to raise money for leatherback sea turtles? Imagine trying to interest people in sea slugs!'"

It was Mike James who, over thirty years later, joined the biological dots sketched out by Bleakney.

Mike started by putting up posters of leatherback turtles in fishing villages across Nova Scotia, asking, "Have you seen this turtle?" It wasn't long before fishermen around the province called in 200 sightings. They also helped Mike locate the incredibly productive jellyfish beds that lure these turtles so far north. They helped him find leatherbacks at sea—not an easy task. Those waters are incredibly big and there are not a lot of leatherbacks out there—remember, they're endangered. It takes what the turtle team calls "good eyes" to find them.

Locating turtles in the wide-open ocean, when they might surface for just a few seconds, takes years of practice. Fishermen also captained their research boat and helped Mike catch turtles so he could attach tracking beacons to their backs. And now, with the help of Kathleen's sea turtle network, the fishermen are learning how to safely release leatherbacks when they get accidentally tangled in their fishing nets, or how to prevent entanglement in the first place.

"It turned out that all those scientists were proven wrong," says Kathleen. "They said there were no sea turtles in Canadian waters. That any odd ones were here by mistake.

In just one summer, the fishermen we started talking to—none of whom had ever been to university—totally changed the face of scientific thinking about leatherback sea turtles. They changed the global understanding of this dinosaur. The fishermen of Nova Scotia did that."

"So what became of Sherman Bleakney?" I ask.

"Oh, he's still alive. He's in his 90's now. What a great and interesting man. A few years ago, we invited him on one of our boats so he could actually *see* a leatherback turtle at sea. That was one of the greatest moments of my life, just watching him watching this turtle. And to think that the research he started so long ago, that nobody supported, became the foundation for all the work we do now. It all came from him."

"What a tale!"

"He's a lovely man. One of my favorites."

(Dr. Bleakney died peacefully on October 25, 2019 in Wolfville, Nova Scotia at the age of 91. His obituary in *The Chronicle Herald* described him as "a diligent researcher and creative thinker who was not afraid to stretch academic boundaries, always with a healthy dose of humor and irreverence. He leaves a legacy of scientific research and publications on everything from leatherback sea turtles to sea slugs; chimpanzee art to the origins of European medieval mollusc symbols . . .")

"Those fishermen," I say, "they're not scientists, but they are so intimate with the sea. They know so many things. What about you, Kathleen? Not a scientist, yet you bring so much to your job."

"As I've moved into this sea turtle work, coming from a wildly different perspective has been really valuable. This stuff is not just cerebral. Along with scientists, I think it's critical that you have writers addressing environmental issues, and artists, filmmakers, and musicians. We have them all on staff. If you really want to change people, you have to absolutely hit them where they're still deeply connected to nature. Where their sense of wonder and curiosity and compassion still lives. You want to be able to get to people's hearts and souls. That's ultimately what we're trying to change here. Then maybe they'll do things to help sea turtles. Or the homeless person on their street. I don't care what they do. If, somehow, we touch them, things will get better."

> "*When* it comes to environmental issues, everybody has something to contribute. Everybody is worthy. You can learn from everybody. There's no one that doesn't have something to give that will astound you.*"

TURTLES FOR CHRISTMAS

"What would you say is your biggest accomplishment?"

"I'm really proud of the fact that a lot more people now think of sea turtles as part of the Canadian ecosystem. People will write to us from across the country, like this lovely group of kids in land-locked Alberta. They love the ocean and want to support us. They can't come out and do beach patrols with us, but they'll hold a bake sale or go door-to-door or do an information booth to raise awareness and money for sea turtles. We have people in Ontario who—I kid you not—send us a box of chocolate turtles each Christmas."

"Hilarious!"

"It's those little, simple things that really add up. It's a huge boost to us. We can feel them cheering for us, and that really helps us do our work. So do their kind donations."

"Other big accomplishments?"

"It's fair to say that our work has shown the critical importance of traditional ecological knowledge in both science and conservation work."

"Your fishermen friends?"

"Yes. There's a million things we couldn't have done without their help and knowledge. I'm super proud of the fine people we've worked with—from my office colleagues, people in tiny fishing communities, and other academics, to little grassroots organizations down in the Caribbean and South America. I'm so proud of these relationships."

"A true network."

"Yes. When I came up with our name, Canadian Sea Turtle *Network*, I chose that word carefully."

According to Kathleen's website (seaturtle.ca), *you*, the reader, are a prime part of that network. She invites you to do a beach patrol to look for stranded turtles, volunteer at their Sea Turtle Centre, packed with "an ocean of discovery," or get down and muddy at one of their environmental camps. Or how about a once-in-a-lifetime field trip to Trinidad to help count, measure, and tag leatherback moms as they arrive on their nesting beaches, or shield hatchlings in their life-and-death scramble to the sea?

Or what about throwing a bake sale? Or sending more chocolate turtles?

Kathleen and her crew will warmly welcome your involvement and support with open arms. These endangered turtles, and the people that help rescue them, need all the help they can get.

I ask Kathleen what personal sacrifices she has made along the way.

"There's no doubt this work has bled into other parts of my life. So much of my time is spoken for. It's rare that I can completely unplug. If there's a sea turtle emergency, I have to get on it. For example, right after I'd given birth to our first child, people were calling the sea turtle hotline next door in the recovery room." Kathleen laughs. "I could hear it ringing. Why was it turned on? I don't know! And I'm thinking, 'Do I answer the phone?'

"I remember another time when my first two children were just tiny. Another full-on emergency, this time a sea turtle stranded on a sand bank. I had to pick them up and head to the South Shore a couple of hours away. They hadn't eaten anything and my son's going, 'We're kind of hungry back here. Do you have any snacks?' And I'm yelling, 'This is a real live animal rescue! We can't stop for snacks. Forget it, you guys! You'll be fine!'"

"Your kids are how old now?"

"Our son Aidan is sixteen, our daughter, Kate, fourteen, and our son, Kieran, nine."

"And are they still connected with your work—willingly or otherwise?"

"Of course they're going to be their own people, but they love all of this. There's a famous story in our family about Aidan's first up-close view of a leatherback turtle. It's a gorgeous evening, the sun is setting. The turtle's lying close to shore and my husband is on a surfboard beside it, saying to him, 'Look, there's a leatherback right in front of you!' And Aidan goes, 'Yeah. Do you have any snacks?' And my husband goes, 'No, sweetie, but look, it's right there!' Aidan says, 'I see it. It's lying there. It's black, it's ...' and he proceeds to describe it perfectly. 'I'm just really hungry.' He's like, 'Whatever,' because this is what he's known his whole life. It's like the work is another member of our family that can get frustrating at times. They make sacrifices, for sure. But all our kids are incredibly supportive of our work."

➤ *Kathleen and young Kate out on the trail*

"Amidst all the great work you're doing, do you fear for the leatherbacks' future?"

"We heard recently that the Atlantic population of leatherback turtles is in decline. That was really chilling for me because I thought, 'Oh my God, we're doing all this stuff! What are we missing? How do we step this up? What more we can do? Like, what's next?' I'm forced to think how we might be failing the turtles, somehow. And that's tough when you're trying your hardest.

"The thing about working with endangered species is you're on a clock, in this case, one that started 100 million years ago. And the population has been decimated in, like, twenty-five years. The stakes are incredibly high, so any bad news can be really worrisome to me."

I ask Kathleen about a Chinese proposal to scoop up Nova Scotia's superabundant jellyfish to feed humans, not turtles. "Is that another looming threat?"

"That hasn't gone anywhere as far as I know. I'm hoping we scared them off! But, yeah, things could go downhill really fast if we're not super careful."

"How do you remain hopeful?"

"I'm not good at creating apocalyptic scenarios. I truly think humanity has this incredible capacity to do things that are surprisingly good as much as surprisingly and depressingly bad. We obviously can't continue on our present trajectory. But I can't even begin to imagine the marvelous things we might choose to do. Maybe that's the relentless optimism of an environmentalist."

"That seems to be a takeaway of so many change-makers I've interviewed for this book. They refuse to dwell on the dark. There's this gushing optimism."

"They've all drunk the same environmental Kool-Aid!" Kathleen says, laughing.

"There's also this passion," I say. "Such different paths, but you're all motivated by a similar passion."

"I think that's really important for young people. There's

no one way. Some people know where they're going, but most don't, and that's kind of more fun. Just do the thing you love.

"When I was in university, writing essays about T. S. Eliot's poem *The Wasteland*, I didn't ever imagine I'd be here. But I'm so glad I am. Really, it's such an honor to work with these ancient creatures, living their lives the way they've done long before humans even existed. It's amazing how beautiful that is. Oh my gosh, I'm so privileged.

"Really, you never know where you're going to land. There are so many ways to use your talents. Just be open to the world, be open to what calls you—even if it's not the thing you ever, ever expected. Witness me, right? And thank goodness for that. What a marvelous surprise my life has been!"

At the heart of Kathleen's zealous devotion to her work is a deep affection for the animals she's been trying to save for over twenty years. In another of her finely crafted blogs, "Turtle Tracks," I sense the boundary blurring between her life and the sea turtles she so loves.

> *"One of the fishermen who captained our field boat for many years once told me that the thing he liked most about leatherbacks was how different each one was. That you could see dozens of them and no two looked quite the same. I think about how important this is—that as humans we remember that animals are individuals, each with their own thoughts and experiences. Their own journeys. Like us."*

TRAILBLAZER TIPS
....

Think globally, act locally
Like those fishermen releasing turtles from their nets, always believe that your small, local actions can change the world. One by one, they can make a huge difference, collectively.

Say it plain
What I first brought to the sea turtle work was communication skills. That's a key tool in any environmental cause—getting the message out clearly, simply, and in an appealing way.

Go multimedia
Don't rely only on bald scientific facts to get your message out. Use a variety of media, like creative writing, art, music, theater, and videos to capture people's hearts, minds, and souls.

Mine the local wisdom
Don't leave it to the "experts" to find solutions to the issue you are working on. Mine the wisdom of local people who may have much to contribute to your cause. We can learn from everybody.

Play the long game
The hardest part of any environmental work can be finding the patience to stick with it, to trust that you're making progress even in the face of huge obstacles or frustrations. Play the long game.

Do what you love
My aunt used to say, "Do what you love, and the money will follow." Find the thing that you really care about, are passionate about, or even just curious about and see where it takes you.

Ask for help

As independent and effective and wonderful as young environmentalists can be, don't hesitate to ask for help from the adults in your world who can give your ideas a boost.

Get some air

Give your innate connection with the natural world room to breathe. Give it oxygen. Go into a forest or park or any natural space and immerse yourself in its soothing power and beauty. The Japanese call it a "tree bath."

"John Theberge is a respected scientist,
a vivid writer, a philosopher, and a fighter."
– Robert Bateman, Naturalist and Artist

"The Theberges come about as close as any
two humans could to knowing the Algonquin
landscape the way a wolf does."
– Monte Hummel, Former President
of World Wildlife Canada

JOHN THEBERGE

Defender of Wolves and Wilderness

Exploring the howling, healing heart of nature

Home: Oliver, British Columbia
Pursuits: Ornithologist, wolf biologist, writer, educator

It started with one book. I was living in Vancouver, my first Christmas away from home, and my brother had sent me Wolves and Wilderness *by some biology professor at the University of Waterloo. My copy of the book is scribbled up and indexed in three colors of ink. On the back cover, the word "Waterloo" is underlined several times. Halfway through the book, I decided I would go there, find this man, and become his student—this man who changed my life.*

Months later, I'm walking with this bush scientist through a sugar maple forest in Algonquin Park, a springtime chorus of songbirds echoing high above our heads. Even as his eyes scan the muddy trail for wolf tracks, he points over his shoulder and says, "Chestnut-sided Warbler." I squint above me, mystified. Later we squish past a marsh. "Northern Waterthrush," he says without looking up, and I'm thinking, What? He knows all these bird songs? I want that!

Forty years later, we're hanging out on his sunny, mountain-view deck. Between us on the glass table is a dusty banker's box full of old notebooks and picture albums. During our long, lazy conversation, John casually calls out the names of unseen birds, singing cheerily all around us.

FROM BUTTERFLIES TO BINOS

John wrote his first field notes when he was eight years old. He penciled them in that loopy, cursive writing they don't teach in school anymore, certainly not in Grade 3. Now everybody keyboards.

I saw a Tiger Swallowtail at 12:15 on the 7 of June, 1949. I saw it in the back yard.

His next entry, from June 24, records his older brother Tom catching a giant silk moth in the school yard. John takes it home in a box, makes a detailed color drawing of it, complete with owlish eyespots on the hindwings, and identifies it correctly—The Polyphemus Moth.

By mid-summer, John has graduated to a fountain pen, labeling his drawing of a Monarch butterfly with enough detail to make any bug scientist blink. Apex, inner margin, scent pouch . . .

"Incredible drawings!" I say.

"One hell of an artist, eh?"

*Sample pages from John's first field journal
started when he was only eight years old*

"You're eight years old, and the anatomy of a butterfly wing is important to you. Where did that come from?"

"My earliest experiences were these nature magazines my mother would read. I'd see pictures of these guys with their butterfly collections and that got my interest going. My mother made a butterfly net for me. My father made me a killing jar with plaster of Paris in the bottom and, of all things, *cy-an-ide,* to kill the butterflies." John laughs in his easy, campfire way. "How about that! Give your kid a bottle of cyanide to play with—isn't that a good idea! So that got me collecting butterflies.

"Then there were the family picnics. My parents had their favorite places north of Oshawa, Ontario, where I grew up. They read books all the time and took them on our picnics. They'd sit quietly under a tree and read, or Dad would go fishing.

"I remember him, coming back from fishing, saying he'd heard this weird bird with a beautiful descending call, but he didn't know what it was. And he'd talk about these giant woodpeckers. So, there was some mystique built up. By the time I was old enough to go with him, I had an interest in birds and realized that the one that so impressed him was a Veery, with its amazing flute-like song. And the giant woodpecker had to be a Pileated. That was a favorite of mine. So, the earliest influences were the family picnics, butterfly collecting, then trout fishing."

"When did your interest in birds take off—so to speak?"

"When I was eleven, a friend of my dad's called up one day and said, 'I'll take your son down to the marsh to see the swan.'"

"The swan?"

John laughs. "The *mute* swan of all things! I don't know if he knew it was an exotic species and, therefore, a curse. He certainly didn't let on if he did. So down we went with his binoculars and he made a big thing of this mute swan. I played along with his excitement. After that, I wanted binoculars to watch birds."

"Now you're hooked."

"The next year when I was twelve, still wanting those binoculars, my father took me to Toronto's Royal Ontario Museum to meet Jim Baillie, of all people."

"You mean the guy behind the famous Baillie Birdathon that raises tons of money for bird conservation?"

"That's him. He was an ornithology hero, the leading bird guy in Ontario in those days. So, we went to his office, and I remember him pulling out drawers full of eye-popping Scarlet Tanager feathers. He made time for a kid who just wanted to know about binoculars, but he went way beyond that to help create my interest in birds. That's one reason he became a conservation hero—because he always had time for people."

"So, you get the binoculars?"

"Yes, I got the binos, and a couple of buddies that I'd hooked on birdwatching. Then they got binoculars and we became a little bird club of three. We had this fun companionship that kids want and need. We'd meet at each other's houses and discuss the birds we saw. We'd all do one field trip a week, make our bird lists, and report back to the others."

"You'd head out on your own?"

"Yes. I'd go off to a secret spot I named 'Warblers Gulch' on Oshawa Creek. It was a great place to learn birds and their songs. My friends went to other places. So, the three of us would have these adventures, sometimes alone, sometimes together."

*Young John (centre) and his birding buddies pumped
for the Christmas Bird Count*

John reaches into a box and thumps a vintage hardcover book onto the glass table. Three trumpeter swans soar across the well-used cover. "About that time, I was much impressed by this book, *Flashing Wings*, by Richard Saunders."

"How so?"

"Saunders was a history professor from London, Ontario, who wrote detailed diaries of each birding trip he went on. This appealed to my sense of outdoor adventure. In the back, there's data on arrival and departure dates for every bird species he mentions. One list is Saunders's, and the other is my friend Jim Baillie's."

"The hotshot birder you saw at the museum."

"Yes, I'd actually *met* that guy, which made this book pretty exciting for me. So, in my young imagination, I felt connected to both of these incredible birders."

"This book was pivotal in your growth as a naturalist?"

"It must have had a major impact on me, because I started writing up my own nature experiences just like he did."

> "*T*he lure of the unexplored, the beckoning finger of novelty—what field naturalist can pass them by? The chance of finding a new bird, a new flower, the hope of having a new experience with some old friend of the wild in a new setting—these are sure enticements to send the ardent naturalist afield in search of adventure."
>
> – Richard Saunders, *Flashing Wings*

BIRDING BUDDIES

It's September 2, 1953. John is twelve years old and about to start Grade 8—his marks let him skip Grade 6. He and a birding buddy, Bill Neal, set out on their bikes for Oshawa Creek amidst rising thunder and an eye-stinging sun shower. It began to "really pour" by the time they entered Warblers Gulch, but the birds didn't seem to mind. As the boys ducked into the woods, John spotted a mixed flock of Canada Warblers, Black-and-white Warblers, and American Redstarts—each species instantly familiar to his trained eye. But then, near the edge of the woods, a mysterious movement in an apple tree. As they stepped closer, three unidentified flying objects darted past them. One landed near enough for John to get a clear shot at it through his binoculars.

LOCAL ENTHUSIASTS TAKE BIRD CENSUS

Newspaper article from January 4, 1955, on the smashing success of John (center) and his birding buddies' first Christmas Bird Count

At first I thought it was just a Robin, John wrote in his field journal, *but the underpart of its tail was toward us. It was black with large white dots on it. I was immediately sure that it was the Yellow-Billed Cuckoo. It suddenly flew, showing the red-brown on the ends of its wings. Then we heard its low, mournful ku-ku-ku-ku-ku. It was really raining with terrific force but we kept in pursuit. Finally, we were driven to put the binoculars in their case. The leaves of the Elm trees were falling rapidly under the heavy rain, when we finally made a mad dash for home. There had been a Cuckoo heard in the district by Mr. Rice, but I was the first to see it. The strange thing was that, two nights previous, I had dreamed of seeing a Cuckoo.*

➤ A passionate young birder, John gets ready for yet another field trip into the woods and wetlands near his Oshawa home.

John described the Cuckoo sighting as "quite an addition" to his fast-growing life list of birds, bringing his total to 112 species. Within a month he would break 120.

I marvel at the carefully typed field notes of this passionate young birder, finding new gems on each pass. Notice his razor-sharp powers of observation (Who looks at the underparts of a bird's tail?), his clear tone of authority ("I was immediately sure ..."), his flair for vivid description ("raining with a terrific force ..."), his openness to the mysterious (the foreshadowing dream of a Cuckoo), and his sensitive eye for nature's beauty (the tumbling Elm leaves). These distinctive hallmarks of John's writing style, already well-established in this twelve-year-old kid, would ripen and gain tremendous power throughout his life.

John's father loved fishing for brook trout in the crystal-clear streams flowing into Lake Ontario. When John was a little kid, he'd be dazzled every time his dad came home from a fishing trip, his creel, or fisherman's basket, brimming with "brookies." Once old enough to join his dad, John couldn't get enough. Those adventures often forced them to wade, waist-deep, across beaver ponds and up rain-choked streams.

➤ *John (L) and friend sport hip waders at a secret fishing hole north of Oshawa.*

September 12, 1953.

Dad and I stepped from the car and picked our way along a little muddy road for the finale of our fishing year. Black clouds were lashed across the sky by a violent wind, occasionally touching the trees as we were high in the ridges. Across a wooden fence lay a small field with tall grass rippling in the wind like a miniature sea. Beyond this, the dense, almost impenetrable woods spread its beckoning hand to us, offering its fishing thrills to anyone who could reach the brook in its heart.

Pulling up our waders, we stepped into the woods, now tramping through a pine-spired forest. Suddenly there was a flash of lightning, a crash of thunder, and rain came pounding down with such a force that it set the woods dancing and trembling.

By now we were in water up to the top of our waders and we spread out to fish. The storm eased and things began to happen fast. Within half an hour, I had creeled seven brookies. The rain stopped and so did the trout.

➤ *Freshly caught trout lie on John's well-used creel basket.*

Suddenly I heard a raucous cry and, looking up, saw a Pileated woodpecker beating rapidly northward, its ruby crown flashing for a brief moment as it looked down over the subjects of its kingdom.

The weight of my filled creel, and the tip of my rod pointing to the orange glow in the clearing sky, were my final impressions of my fishing year.

Here's another typed journal entry from the wild fringe of town. You won't find anything about birds, butterflies, or brook trout in John's field report—just the arresting beauty of a twilight walk with his father in early autumn.

September 18, 1953
Today the signs of fall were prominent everywhere I looked. Many of the small Sumac and other shrubs were in their fall dress of brilliant reds and bright oranges. But the fall began for me as Dad and I were walking home from town in the soft darkness. Suddenly the heavens were a blaze of glory. The green Northern Lights were shooting across the sky. What made this show most spectacular was a Cedar tree outlined by the light, and the black clouds making a perfect continuation of it in the sky. This is a sight I will not forget in a long time.

And here's John, a few weeks later, wandering the piney hills north of Oshawa along the Oak Ridges Moraine. His family is hiking to a hidden cabin in the woods on a "beautiful sunny afternoon." In this entry you can sense the first budding of his personal conservation ethic, which declares that people who "see no beauty" in nature will eventually despoil it.

October 13, 1953.
The woods on our way were wonderful to behold. There was much more color in the trees than I have ever seen. After driving on a gravel road winding through the glorious woods—that have not yet been spoiled by the people who see no beauty in them—we began to walk up a small cart trail overgrown with weeds. Tom had given me a new compass for my birthday, so I was intent on seeing if I could make out our course so we could follow it back.

"So many field trips," I say. "You're just out there enjoying and learning about nature. But did you ever get the feeling, as a kid, that the natural world might be in big trouble?"

"I don't think so. It was a different age. I think a young person today could hardly escape that feeling. But for me, it wasn't till the 'Second Marsh' issue hit the news."

"Tell me about that."

John pulls out a dog-eared newspaper article from the *Oshawa Times*, showing a picture of a dead swan in a marsh.

"Is that the same mute swan that Don Rice showed you?"

"I think so," John says, and starts reading the article. "*Swan found dead in marsh. A familiar and beloved figure, missing today from the Oshawa waterfront. For five years the bird has been seen locally at all times of the year, especially in winter. It first appeared here with a mate that was shot by a hunter. The swan stayed on but eventually died from suspected poison picked up from the bottom of the Second Marsh.*"

"That's *the* swan that got you so fired up," I say, "and led to your first pair of binoculars. And there it is, poisoned. Did this fan the flames of your passion for conservation?"

John tells me how the Oshawa shoreline was once blessed with three bird-rich wetlands, but the so-called "Third Marsh" was already threatened by the construction of a massive harbor for ocean-going boats steaming through the St. Lawrence Seaway. "So, yes, my first campaign was to save the Second Marsh. I wrote my first newspaper article about saving it. My friends and I plotted out where there should be a nature trail and some sort of nature house built inside the marsh. We presented an alternative plan to the port authority. That was my first shot at it."

Today, Second Marsh is the largest remaining urban wetland along Canada's most densely populated lakeshore. Join the dots backward and eventually you'll hit on the conservation campaign that young John got rolling so many decades ago.

> "*O*nce you establish an emotional connection to nature, environmental activism is a natural by-product.*"

CLUB TIME

By the time John was in Grade 10, his passion for birds had overflowed beyond his hometown of Oshawa to the Toronto-based Federation of Ontario Naturalists, who wrote him a letter in November 1954, encouraging him to start a local nature club.

John reads me the letter. "*Dear Mr. Theberge. We have heard of your interest in natural history and the formation of your junior naturalist club . . .*" John laughs. "That's just the three of us! . . . *To this end we have included a guide to forming naturalist clubs by Dr. W. H. Gunn.*"

"You mean, *the* Bill Gunn?" I ask, remembering when I was a kid, listening to his classic nature record, "A Day in Algonquin Park," over and over till I almost wore through the vinyl.

"Yep," John laughs. "Another Canadian conservation hero . . . *We wish you and your club every success . . ."*

Success came a few weeks after that letter, with a phone call to John from the *Oshawa Times.* A reporter wanted to get the scoop on Oshawa's first Christmas Bird Count, organized by John and his small flock of birding buddies.

"I did an interview with this woman and told her the names of all the birds we'd counted. When they came out in the newspaper, they had *Ruffled Grouse,* instead of Ruffed Grouse, and *Harry Woodpecker* for Hairy Woodpecker." John laughs. "She was not an ornithologist! Our family friend Don Rice saw the article and came back into the picture. He told us, 'Yes, let's go ahead with this naturalist's club. I'll do everything I can to make it happen.' He took on the role of President because we were just kids and didn't know what to do with this thing we'd helped start."

"That newspaper article was the spark?"

"Yes, but all that was an outgrowth from the day Don Rice took me down to the marsh to see that mute swan."

"Hurray for mute swans!" I say.

They called it the Oshawa Naturalist's Club—and it's still going strong over sixty years later.

"As a sort of thank-you for getting the club going, I was

ARE YOU INTERESTED IN

BIRDS?

WOODS?

STREAMS?

FIRST MEETING OF THE
OSHAWA FIELD-NATURALISTS
TUESDAY, MARCH 29th

ANIMAL LIFE?

made the program chairman. The three of us were the official producers of the newsletter. We were good friends and had a lot of fun putting it together. We called it *Nature News and Notes*."

"How did that work?"

"We'd meet in one of our houses and pick some sort of theme, like birds of prey, or migration. There was stuff on field trips, bird observations, meetings. We hand-drew the whole thing on a stencil that we took to a neighbor, who had a printing press in his basement."

John pulls out a stack of curling brown newsletters. "Probably nobody else has the whole set. Look at this, Volume 1, number 1!"

The first issue invites nature lovers to a special May long-weekend at Willow Beach, a sweet sprawl of sand and juicy bird habitat east of Oshawa. Star hosts for the celebration included none other than master birder, Jim Baillie, and a government biologist named Dave Fowle.

John describes that weekend as a "confirming time" for him as a naturalist, with "all these people around me with similar interests." But it was Fowle who had the biggest impact.

"We went on all the birding field trips—I saw my first Palm Warbler that weekend and a bunch more. Then came the final count. So up got Dave Fowle, a big tree behind him, all of us in front of him on the beach. He's reading through his bird list, and people are shouting, 'Yeah, got that one!' and in the middle he says, 'There's a Warbling Vireo singing behind me.' And then he casually carries on down the list. He didn't even look up and he nailed it—a Warbling Vireo! And I thought, *'Wow! He knows all the birds by song? I want to be like that!'*"

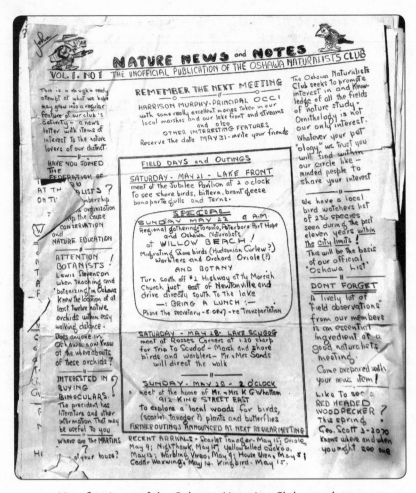

*Very first issue of the Oshawa Naturists Club newsletter,
produced by John and his birding buddies*

"*Living in a sustainable way begins with an
inquisitive mind searching for an understanding
of the workings of the natural world. Understanding
how nature works will increase our love of nature
and make us better stewards of it.*"

After a break for lunch and a quick birding walk around John's pine-studded property, he picks up his story from a new angle: Scouting.

"You know how when you have an older brother who ploughs the way for you? Tom did that for me in Scouts. We had two first-rate leaders who took us to this wonderful scout camp on a big chunk of land north of Oshawa. Camp Samac. It was quite wild, with forest paths everywhere, a creek, a big pond to practice canoeing, even a swimming pool. We'd play wide-ranging games like 'Hounds and Hares' and 'Capture the Flag.' The adventure was a big part of the experience.

"I remember, once, our leaders sitting in the dining hall talking about seeing a flock of Blue-winged Teal swerving through the air in unison, showing the brilliant blue flash of their wings. These two young guys were *really* impressed with this simple sighting. And somehow that little nothing moment had a big impact on my young imagination.

"Inspired by those leaders, I went as far as I could go in scouting, moving up through the badges to Queen's Scout. I was fifteen when I got my first job—a camp woodcraft instructor. There wasn't a lot of woodcraft that summer, but we did build an open-air chapel."

"Is the camp still there?"

"Now it's mostly surrounded by city. But Camp Samac is alive and well to this day. It was definitely a formative place for me."

"What became of your naturalist club?"

"There were a few years of status quo—the three of us buddies doing *Nature News and Notes*, continuing our bird hikes at Warblers Gulch, learning all the time. As the program guy, I would line up speakers for our club meetings. My parents would ask them over for dinner and then we'd go to the club."

"I love how your parents kindled your passion by inviting these people over for dinner to hear their stories."

"Yep, they definitely did."

"What was that like for you?"

John laughs. "I was generally in awe! After being amazed by Dave Fowle . . ."

"The bird-by-ear guy at your beach party?"

"Right. I got the bright idea of asking Fowle to come speak to our club. I'd hit him up for a summer job when he came over for dinner."

"You're about to graduate from high school?"

"Yes. I was seventeen in Grade 13."

Fowle's letter arrived a few days after their family dinner together. John reads it to me, ending with the announcement that, ". . . *The only position we have available is with the wolf research program.*"

"Only *wolves*, John?" I say, laughing. "Too bad!"

MEETING A MENTOR

Dave Fowle had assigned John to work with wolf biologist, Doug Pimlott, who would quickly become John's main mentor and inspiration. Here's their first meeting as described in a tribute John wrote about Doug twenty years later.

I met Doug in 1959 when I had the good fortune, upon finishing high school, to land a summer job with Ontario's new wolf research program. It was a hot July day. I had been assigned the mundane task of transferring data collected about bountied wolves onto punch cards, when Doug walked in, fresh from

John's main mentor and inspiration, wolf biologist Doug Pimlott

Algonquin Park. He introduced himself, then sat down at a desk piled high with unopened mail. I did not realize, then, how that man would change my life, shape my career, and build for me a conservation ethic to live by.

Many people have felt the force of his personality emanating from the lecture platform, or conference room, or the pages of his writing. I count myself lucky to have felt it in the wilderness, beside the campfire, listening to or watching wolves.

Lucky for John, Doug relieved him of the boring office work and sent him north to a wildlife research station in the heart of lake-studded Algonquin Park. Though John was still paid only $6.50 a day, the rewards were huge. "It was a really exciting, stimulating place to work. There was a team of admirable biologists up there who, for a young guy like me, were heroes. There were also other young people in training. We had our good times and our parties, then everybody would disperse back to their labs or their field work. Everybody worked very hard on their projects. The whole experience shaped me. But Doug shaped me even more."

When the party was over, what project did John return to? Cleaning wolf heads.

"The heads of all those wolves I'd been punching cards for had been frozen and shipped to the wildlife station."

"What did you actually *do* with their heads?"

"My job was to clean everything out with a toothbrush. It all had to go—hair, ears, eyes, brains."

"Marvelous. And *why* were you doing this?"

"Taxonomy. Even then there was some sense that there was something different about the wolves up there. People did detailed measurements of the skulls after I boiled and cleaned them."

"You *boiled* the heads? Over a fire?"

"Yeah. I used a big old bathtub that some Prince had enjoyed long ago in a local hotel. They were all wrapped in cheesecloth, thrown in boiling water for five, six, seven hours until the meat would just fall off and you could stir out the brains. I'd wash them up with a toothbrush, clamp their teeth together, and stack them out to dry on big racks that I'd made in a clearing."

"What a weird scene. All those leering skulls. Right out of Shakespeare!"

"Just imagine me sitting there with those wolf skulls boiling, and the fire and the smoke, the steam and the stench. Everybody made fun of me when I came to meals in the cookhouse. They'd go and sit on the other side of the table.

"But I was told, if I got those darned skulls done, I'd get to go out in the field and study wolves with Doug. So, I worked day and night. I kept that fire going all the time. I was boiling them like hell."

All that sweat and stink paid off. Impressed by John's

In those early days at Doug Pimlott's side, John admits that
"we didn't know anything about wolf howling."

dogged determination to finish such a gruesome task, Doug invited him into the field to howl up some wolves.

"Back then, nobody had any idea how to locate and count wolves in wilderness areas. Doug had this idea of broadcasting recorded wolf howls into the bush and getting wolves to howl back. We went out together, that very first time, down a logging road near Lake Louisa, where loggers had told us they'd heard wolves howl when they turned off their chainsaws. We hauled out all our untested gear—the wolf tapes, the recorder, a big speaker mounted on top of the truck. Doug said, 'I'll go up the hill to listen. You play the recording, and we'll see what happens.'

"So, I'm in the truck. It's getting dark. I hit 'play' and it turns out we were right on top of the wolves! They all howled back. Suddenly Doug comes crashing back through the brush. We didn't know what we'd done, whether we would be attacked or what."

"You didn't know?"

"In those days, we didn't know anything about wolf howling. Nobody knew what would happen when you played a howl at point blank range. But we didn't get attacked and realized this was a promising technique. Doug invited me back the next summer to do it again. And again. He hired a skilled old woodsman, Lawrence, and a young college guy, me, and sent us off, over a huge block of Algonquin Park, to find and count wolves. And away we went!"

WOLF HUNT

Indeed, away they went, in Doug's red cedar-strip canoe, searching for wolves in the wild. In his first book, *Wolves and Wilderness*, John wrote about his research adventures with Lawrence, a seasoned bush man who "could find a portage that would baffle an otter." One of my favorite scenes is the night they discovered they could communicate directly with wolves, voice to voice.

This was success. We had found our first wolves and they were answering us. A chill ran up my spine and into the back of my neck as I listened to the indescribable beauty of that wild chorus and realized that it was their answer to our vocal howling, not to the mirrored sound of the tape player. We had been accepted by the creature which, above all others, symbolizes the spirit of wilderness.

Doug Pimlott knew well that, as John writes, the wolf is "the most loved and hated of North American mammals." Doug told him that "the future of the wolf depends on people finding positive and interesting things about them." He had a theory that howling offered the best way into people's hearts and sent John out to test it.

"I was no screaming wonderful academic when I met Doug. But he was good at recognizing potential and slotting people into things he thought they could handle. Like the undergraduate project he helped me with on wolf howling."

"What was that about?"

"I distributed howling forms to park campsites, lodges, all over the place. I told people, 'If you've heard howling, please fill this out.' Then I collected the forms, *lots* of them. People wrote all over them! They'd heard wolves howl and it was obviously a huge, exciting thing for them. It really was a breakthrough. So, Doug was right. Howling *was* a way to change the way people see wolves."

Under Doug's guiding hand at the University of Toronto, John went on to pursue graduate studies on wolves, "to learn their language—why they howl, and what they say." After John finished his PhD, Doug helped him land his first teaching job at the University of Waterloo. "He slotted me there, too," John says. "Then one day he said, 'I'm giving you my Algonquin wolf work. And here's my red canoe.'"

John's beloved mentor and friend was dying.

"Doug assigned things to people when he knew he was going to die." Along with a freezer full of unanalyzed wolf scats (John never did find them), Doug entrusted him with decades of data from his pioneering wolf research that he knew John could handle.

Once again, Doug was right about John.

"This string of wolf data from Algonquin is the longest in Canada," John says. Picking up where Doug left off, he helped identify a new species of wolf found mainly in Algonquin

John gently radio-collars an Algonquin wolf to track its movements in and out of the park.

Park (Remember all those wolf heads?). They called it the Algonquin wolf, *Canis rufus,* or Red wolf, thought to be a close cousin of the original ancestor of *all* wolves. Due to its threatened status, and intensive wolf hunting and trapping near the park, John successfully fought and won a battle to create a unique no-kill zone around the whole park.

"That's something I'm very proud of," John tells me as he looks back on the legacy of his career. Thanks, in a huge way, to John's work, Algonquin has become a world-famous wolf sanctuary. Over the decades since his howling good times with Doug Pimlott, more people have learned about wolves and heard them howl in Algonquin Park than anywhere else on Earth.

John also points to his role in creating Yukon's Kluane National Park, a spectacular stronghold protecting Canada's tallest mountains. "That was big. And I have to say I'm also proud of the students I helped and, in turn, the legacy they leave. There are people like you, who I know about. But there were a lot of faceless people in those classes who've since told me I changed their careers. So, they weren't all asleep!" John says, laughing. "That makes me feel really good."

"And all your books, John."

"And my books. But I love to write, just as you do, so that's not work, that's pleasure. Hopefully there's an influence there, too."

So why *do* wolves howl? This remains one of John's favorite scientific mysteries, which he still explores today with his research partner, co-author, artist, and wife, Mary. "I would never have built the career I've had without Mary. We've done our work together, along the same path. Mary's been the driver of a lot of our work. She's the

strategist. She's not as hot-headed as I am and has stopped me from doing a few stupid things along the way!"

From their book, *Wolf Country—Eleven Years Tracking the Algonquin Wolves*, here's the intrepid couple, having paddled back into camp just before midnight after a fruitless search for radio-collared wolves:

Then, at 3:15 am, the wolves found us, their howls gradually impressing themselves on our awareness. I climbed out of the tent for a bearing. A waning moon hung just above the mist still lying over the marsh. Silvery dewdrops clung to the tips of pine needles outlined with clarity in the moonlight. Both collared wolves were there, out along the creek where we had been. They howled on and on, long after I returned to the tent. We lay still and listened.

Months after John reluctantly packed up his ancient field notes and bird lists, his dog-eared clippings and newsletters, wondering "what to do with all this stuff," he called me to say that he'd shown some of these "relicts" to his ten-year old grandson, who "ate it up." His grandson has started to keep his own bird lists. They're going birding together for the first time. And maybe soon, when they're in the right place at the right time, they'll go howling for wolves.

> **"T**oday the howl reminds us that our past is deep-rooted in wildness. It warns us not to go too far in destroying natural environments. It epitomizes the wilderness we have fought so successfully to conquer and now must fight to save.**"**

TRAILBLAZER TIPS
....

Find adventure
The only way to hook people on nature is through recreation and enjoyment. With kids it's adventure. You can't hook them on philosophy or ethics. It's the adventure that grabs them.

Learn, learn, learn
To tackle a conservation issue, first learn everything you can. In advocacy work, knowledge is power. We succeeded in protecting the Algonquin wolves because we had the data, the power.

Balance head and heart
Understanding how nature works will increase our emotional connection to nature. Environmental activism is a natural by-product of both knowledge and feelings, head and heart.

Be patient
It takes time to find solutions to environmental problems. Don't jump right in, thinking you can change the world. Be patient. Trust in yourself and others working on your cause. Don't give up.

Make cool connections
Building support for an issue depends on finding something positive and interesting that gets people's attention. Public interest in howling helped save the wolves of Algonquin Park.

Don't let your guard down
In the conservation game, there's no such thing as a permanent victory. Celebrate your successes. But don't let your guard down. Stay vigilant, else you may lose them quickly.

Find companions

If you have a special interest or issue, find kindred companions to share it—like my birding buddies when I was young. They'll give you energy, focus, and momentum. And it's more fun.

Get outside

In our urbanized, technologized, highly structured lives, it gets harder to get outside. Go roll in a bog, camp by a stream, or just walk in a park to connect with nature and regain perspective.

Mary, John, and Jamie at the Theberges' mountainside home in May, 2018

"These kids see no reason to wait until they are older to make a difference in the world."

– Mother Nature Network

"Rupert and Franny are incredible volunteers for the environmental rights movement."

– David Suzuki Foundation

RUPERT & FRANNY YAKELASHEK

No Minimum Age Required

Fighting for environmental rights,
one government at a time

Home: Victoria, British Columbia
Pursuits: Environmental rights, youth advocacy

I first heard about Rupert and Franny Yakelashek on Starfish Canada's "Top 25 Environmentalists Under 25" web page. They were the youngest among the award winners that year, 2017, just thirteen and ten years old. Their bios described them as courageous, tenacious, passionate, hard-working, and "radiating optimism." As I read on, I was amazed to learn that they were already veteran activists, working on environmental campaigns they had launched three years earlier when Franny was seven and Rupert ten. A quick scan of online news stories about them gave me an instant itch to get to know these super siblings from Victoria, B.C.

A CALL TO ACTION

When introducing me to their Victoria home, Franny and Rupert Yakelashek are quick to point out the cultural and natural backdrop on which it sits.

"We're growing up on the traditional homeland of the Esquimalt and Songhees First Nation people," Rupert says. "We feel really lucky to live in Victoria, surrounded by such beautiful landscapes."

"It really is one of the most natural places in the whole world," Franny tells me. "We've got ocean, forests, rivers, mountains, and lakes all around us. Nature has always been a big thing for us."

➤ *"We're surrounded by so much natural beauty. We play on the beaches, swim the lakes, hike the trails."*

As a little kid, Franny loved to explore anywhere outside, go biking with her dad, play on local beaches, grow food in her garden, and take care of her chickens, Daisy, Rose, and Poppy. And, of course, Fennel, her pet rabbit.

Rupert describes his younger self as a "science adventurer," eating up any tidbit of science and nature he could sink his teeth into. "My parents would always make sure my pants and coats had lots of pockets to hold my compass, magnifying glass, and all the treasures I came across on my travels—like rocks, feathers, and other bits and pieces from the outdoors." Watching science and nature shows was another one of Rupert's passions as a kid. He says the lore he picked up from those experiences comes in handy when exploring today's environmental issues, whether global or local.

Franny and Rupert call themselves "homelearners." Their education is served up by a close family, good friends, and the local home-schooling community. A cornerstone of their curriculum is making a positive impact on their community and the world. "And we have a lot of fun!" says Franny. "We love to spend time at home being cozy. It's safe to say we're all introverts in our family, but we also love going out and having adventures."

The seed for a new kind of adventure was planted one day in the fall of 2014, when ten-year-old Rupert was studying Grade 5 Civics. Though intimately connected to the natural world, he learned from his teacher that when the environment needs protection, children have the absolute *least* power to do anything about it.

What a blow for a boy so nuts about nature!

Still bummed by this bad news, Rupert and Franny had the course of their lives change a few days later by a simple call to action from environmental icon, David Suzuki. He was hosting a splashy public event promoting his Blue Dot campaign, a grassroots movement guaranteeing every Canadian's right to enjoy a healthy environment and have a say in how it's protected.

Blue Dot beach party!

Franny and Rupert learned that a great way to make this happen would be for all levels of government—from town councils to the federal parliament—to pass an Environmental Rights Declaration that would help ramp up environmental laws, clean up polluted air and water, and bump up environmental awareness among both politicians and the public.

This sure sounded good to them.

But then came more bad news.

They learned that, of the 110 countries around the world that had entrenched their citizens' environmental rights in laws or constitutions, Canada was not one of them.

Rupert couldn't believe his ears. "I was flabbergasted that Canada didn't have environmental rights. I'd always thought of Canada as a very environmentally friendly place. It was shocking to think that our government's priorities were just completely wrong. Politicians are worried about losing the next election instead of actually preserving our rich land for people to live in. This should be the highest priority of any government anywhere. You only get one chance to save the world and keep it healthy."

Just seven years old, Franny, too, was sad to learn that, even in a rich country like Canada, some kids her own age had to live with dirty water or stinky air.

As the upbeat talks and music wound down at Suzuki's Blue Dot party, the audience was invited to join the movement and become environmental rights champions. Rupert and Franny were ready to volunteer on the spot.

Environmental rights means a healthy planet for future generations
— Rupert

But there was just one catch.

They figured they were too young.

VICTORY IN VICTORIA

After the buzz of the Blue Dot blast-off, Rupert remembers asking himself, "What can I do to help? I'm just a kid. I can't vote. I can't choose the politicians I want."

Rupert felt powerless. So he turned to his main home-school teacher for help. "Me and my mom brainstormed ideas."

And they hatched a clever plan.

With a November municipal election just weeks away, voting fever was sweeping through the streets of Victoria. Choosing politicians who supported the idea of environmental rights could help kick-start the cause Rupert and Franny now firmly believed in. So what if they couldn't vote? That didn't mean they couldn't influence those who could.

"We decided to write letters to candidates for the Victoria election," Rupert tells me. "We went to the all-candidates meet-and-greet and handed our letters to the candidates, saying: if you promise to make this declaration, we'll convince our parents and all the other adults we know to vote for you.

Lots of the candidates agreed, and Franny and I set to work to get them elected. And most of them were!"

➤ *At age seven, Franny was already a veteran political letter writer.*

After helping to stack Victoria's City Council with politicians who, at least, *said* they supported their cause, Franny and Rupert kept up the pressure, lobbying them to pass a formal Environmental Rights Declaration.

Back when the Yakelashek siblings got bit by the environmental rights bug, only a handful of Canadian cities had passed declarations: Vancouver, Montreal, Yellowknife, Richmond, B.C., and The Pas, Manitoba. Franny and Rupert aimed to make Victoria the next.

In the weeks that followed, Rupert and Franny did their homework, learning all they could about environmental rights and how to be better activists. They hand-delivered more letters to councilors, demanded meetings with city officials, and held interviews with local media. They politely pushed themselves onto the agenda for the December 18, 2014, Council meeting at Victoria's City Hall. The question on the floor: to pass or not to pass an Environmental Rights Declaration.

There were presentations to write, posters to prepare, and a public rally to arrange.

Yes, a rally. Under the City Hall bell tower.

It began at 6:45 PM, just before the Council meeting, precisely as all the councilors, city staff, reporters, and the public streamed into City Hall. They called it Rupert's Rally for a Healthy Environment. "Kids need to be heard," Rupert yelled at the rally, "and municipal governments have some of the biggest impacts on people!" The rally set the tone for the rest of the evening: This is a kid-led proposal, folks, and you need to take it seriously.

Four years later, I ask Franny about the hardest thing she's ever done. She tells me it happened that night, speaking as a seven-year-old, to a packed Council chamber.

"I've done a lot of challenging things, but the hardest thing I ever did was make that first speech. It was also the scariest. I was a very, very shy kid. I was so shy I barely spoke, and when I did, I was very quiet."

Hi! My name is Franny. I am 7 years old.

I am here because the environment is important to me. I love the beauty of nature and nature itself.

Last month I went on a nature scavenger hunt at Government House hosted by David Suzuki. I was reminded that humans can't survive with out a healthy environment.

I think it is important that Victoria makes a declaration for environmental rights so every one knows how important it is to take care of the world that keeps us alive.

Thank you for listening.

Franny's "terrifying" public speech in front of Victoria's City Council

"I had never written a speech, I could barely read, and the thought of speaking in public was terrifying. But I wanted our city to pass an Environmental Rights Declaration, so I pushed myself to do it. My speech was color-coded to help me. All the environmental words were printed in green; all the complicated words I'd practiced were in pink. I had my favorite stuffed animal with me."

"And who was that?"

"Toni, my fuzzy dog. She went everywhere with me, I mean *everywhere*. She's met a lot of interesting people and has even made the front page of our newspaper. Even now, I'll take her with me sometimes when I need a little extra support for a big speech or something."

Franny clutches Toni, her favorite stuffy, who helped her find the courage to make that first speech—and many since.

"So, there you were at seven years old for your *first* big speech. You're clutching Toni. You're on pins and needles, about to take on City Hall."

"My mom, Skye, stood beside me. I stepped up onto a chair and spoke as loud as I could into the microphone to the mayor, all the councilors, and a full council chamber. I let them know how I felt, how everyone deserves a healthy environment. I told them what I wanted."

Both kids spoke to a hushed audience. Everyone listened carefully, not wanting to miss a word from the lips of these young eco-warriors. Many were moved to tears.

Their message was simple: Protect the land and water that give us life. Always think about kids when you make decisions about the future. Legally recognize environmental rights. And, always remember that kids' voices count!

In the end, the vote was unanimous. The mayor and all eight councilors gave the thumbs-up to Franny and Rupert's proposal.

➤ *Spreading their environmental message during a CBC radio interview*

"I was thrilled!" says Franny. "And so proud of myself for being brave. We got what we wanted. Victoria officially recognized everyone's right to live in a clean environment. It was a huge confidence booster!"

And how did Rupert feel after their victory? "I couldn't speak! I was speechless for the first time in my life! When I got home, I had to eat four bowls of ice cream to recover."

Thanks to their creative and compelling campaign, Victoria did indeed become the next community in Canada to pass an Environmental Rights Declaration. Rupert and Franny had spearheaded a movement that was about to go viral across the country. Today, over 150 Canadian towns and cities have signed on. A bunch of those were inspired to do so after receiving a knock on the door or a letter in the mail from Rupert and Franny Yakelashek.

> "*E*nvironmental rights are a human right. This means all people have the inalienable right—it can't be taken away—to clean air, clean water, healthy food, diverse ecosystems. It means they have the right to help make environmental decisions that may impact them. And they have the right to demand justice whenever a healthy environment is threatened."

CASTING THE NET

After their electrifying victory in Victoria, Rupert and Franny set their sights on what's called the Capital Region District,

*Franny and Rupert's letter-writing campaign inspired
Environmental Declarations in towns across B.C., and beyond.*

including over a dozen cities, towns, and islands next door
to Victoria. Out went the letters, in came the invitations—to
attend council meetings in over half of the communities
they'd contacted.

Then they cast their net even wider, writing to every
municipality on Vancouver Island. In the end, they snagged
23 communities, getting them to pass environmental rights
declarations on the island, and inspiring similar declarations
across B.C. in Smithers, Masset, and Powell River.

The media loved Rupert and Franny. Their fame spread.
They started getting invitations to conferences.

Rupert remembers well his speech at the Union of B.C.
Municipalities conference. "I was eleven years old when they
invited me to speak. When I showed up, they told me that I
was the *keynote* speaker—and the *only* speaker. I was totally
taken aback. Was I ready to speak to this huge room full of
municipal and provincial leaders?

"Then guess who arrived—David Suzuki! Only a year had passed since I'd sat in the audience, learning about environmental rights from Dr. Suzuki and his Blue Dot Team. This was a great opportunity to show what I'd learned and how I'd grown into an environmental rights advocate since that inspiring night. I was totally nervous, but I gave my presentation, and I think everyone was inspired."

Rupert convinced the conference delegates to vote "Yes" for a province-wide declaration of environmental rights. "After that speech, I felt I could do just about anything!"

Among the inspired listeners that day was Suzuki himself. "For me, listening to Rupert and witnessing his leadership was extra special," he writes in an online Blue Dot article, "Growing environmental leadership fills me with gratitude ... Rupert got his start one year ago when the Blue Dot Tour landed in Victoria. I launched the tour with the hope that we would inspire Canadians to stand up for a better vision for our future ... Rupert was listening in the audience in Victoria, and he swung into action from that day. And here I was, one year later, listening to him speak to me about the need to protect our right to a healthy environment. It was inspiring to see the idea of environmental rights come full circle."

Another conference invitation came from the Responsible Investment Association, a group of wealthy bankers and financial planners who believe that everyone should think about environmental and social concerns when they invest their dollars. Rupert and Franny were flown to Toronto and put up in a fancy hotel. They opened the conference with a panel discussion: "Talking About Tomorrow: Conversations with Today's Youth Leaders." They spoke to 450 investment professionals, dressed in their business best, about everything from plastic pollution to Indigenous culture, and, of course, environmental rights. The youth panel received a storm of applause among all those big-shot money managers looking for a better way forward.

No strangers to the podium, Franny and Rupert speak in San Francisco after receiving an International Eco-Hero Award.

Not satisfied with their wave of successes at the municipal and corporate levels, Rupert and Franny started pounding on the doors of higher halls of power. These days, their environmental rights campaigns are aimed at the provincial and federal governments. More letters, more speeches, more interviews, more meetings, now with Members of Parliament, party leaders, and Ministers of Environment, all aimed at pushing environmental rights legislation across Canada.

"Where we live," says Franny, "we're surrounded by so much natural beauty. We play on the beaches, swim the lakes, hike the trails. We know some Canadian kids aren't so lucky. Like people who live around Sarnia, Ontario. They call it

Speaking at a youth-led rally on the steps of Victoria's provincial Parliament buildings during the Global Climate Strike of March 2019

Chemical Valley because the air and water are so polluted. And what about the Indigenous people of Canada's north, trying to adapt to climate change? It makes me sad to think of so many other examples. This should not be happening in Canada. Every kid in this country should be able to live without worrying about pollution or climate change."

I ask Rupert how they hope to reach this lofty goal.

"We're working with other environmental rights advocates and Blue Dot volunteers, asking national leaders to make a Federal Bill of Environmental Rights. That way, every Canadian child and their families could live in a safe and healthy environment.

"There's still a lot of work, but we're motivated to do what we can to make positive change. Ultimately, we'd like to see environmental rights recognized in the Canadian Charter of Rights and Freedoms!"

JUST REGULAR KIDS
·······································

When asked by a journalist why all this mattered, here's what Rupert said: "This matters to me because I'm doing it for my future, and other kids' futures. Adults are making decisions that affect *our* future, but most of them won't even be here to experience the consequences."

Another journalist once asked him what it feels like to have adults listen to him and take action. "I felt that I wasn't powerless and that I deserved to be heard. Although City Council meetings aren't usually attended by children, when they do, the politicians pay attention. You don't need to be special to make a change. I want kids to feel like they have a voice, because they *do*. They're the ones that will inherit the future. You can never be too young to start making the world that you want."

Rupert and Franny call themselves, "environmental rights advocates and changemakers—or regular kids trying to make positive change." Ever since their victory in Victoria, when they were only ten and seven, they have been fighting against the myth that "regular kids" *can't* make a positive change.

I ask them why their peers might feel this way.

"Many young people feel that advocacy and activism are only for adults," says Franny. "They just accept this, but it's not true. Kids and youth *can* make real change in their families, school, community, and world! The more you look around, the more stories you see about young people standing up for what they believe in. We need to share those stories and let all young people know they can start creating the world they want and need."

Making waves on the front pages of local media

Rupert blames "over-scheduled lives, the prevalence of technology and screen-based interactions, and too little time in nature as obstacles preventing young people from stepping up to be environmental changemakers. In my opinion, to really feel empowered to tackle environmental challenges, kids need more open schedules, more experiences in nature, and more relationships with encouraging people."

He feels that even when young people are inspired to act, adults can get in the way. "We feel many adults underestimate youth and our capacity to make change. Often we're treated like we're not responsible enough, educated enough, skilled enough, or experienced enough to tackle issues that directly impact our future."

"What advice do you have for kids who want to make a difference?" I ask.

"First of all," says Franny, "you need to believe in yourself. Figure out what's important to you, what you want to change and how you're going to do it. Make an action plan, then work very hard to meet your goal. If the project's too big for one person, find others to join you. Our experience is that people are happy to give advice, share ideas, offer resources and time, or help you develop the skills you need. No one expects young people to have all the answers, so be humble and ask for help."

"My advice," says Rupert, "is take the first step toward making change, no matter how small. Each step creates a ripple. If everyone took small steps, then together we'd make big waves. Every little bit helps. And when you can, do more!"

"How do you know you've made a difference?"

"Me and Rupert's advocacy work has gone way past what we can measure," says Franny. "I know we're making a difference because that's what's been communicated back to us. People from all over Canada and the world have reached out, asking for information, sending invitations, or just letting us know they're inspired by our work. If we motivate *anyone* to take action, that's a sign we've made a difference."

Rupert says it's really hard to measure if you've made a difference. "But what I'm doing is meaningful to me, so, even if I'm just making small changes in the world, it's making a big change in me, and that's what's important."

Here's the world "communicating back" to Franny and Rupert through a heap of environmental awards: an international Gloria Barron Prize for Young Heroes, a Nature Inspiration Award from the Canadian Museum of Nature, a National Top 25 Environmentalists Under 25 award, and an Honorary Citizen's Award from their home town of Victoria.

All well-earned.

They both believe that part of getting fellow youth pumped about environmental activism is packaging it in fun ways. One of their lures is to blend activism with art in kid-friendly workshops and classes. Topics include hand-drawn comics to explain environmental rights or the mysteries of government, how to write change-making letters, or create murals to explore what makes a healthy environment. They helped organize an art class at Victoria's main art gallery to explore environmental and indigenous rights—an exhibit that later went public for all to see.

Accepting Honorary Citizen's Awards from the City of Victoria

Their latest dream is to create a comic book or graphic novel that would educate young people about environmental rights and how to use them to protect their future. "We're still working out how to do this," says Franny.

Knowing these guys, they'll make it happen.

"**W**e understand why so many children feel powerless to make a change, or disengage altogether. The world is ruled by adults. But it will be children who inherit the consequences of today's decisions, good and bad. So, we need to stand up now to start creating and protecting the world we want, need, and deserve."

WHAT'S THE FORECAST?

I feel privileged to ask these bright-eyed, hard-nosed young activists about a future that I may never see. "How is the world going to look by middle of this century?"

"There are still many people who see the planet as a way just to make money," says Rupert "Everything's a resource, a commodity. This is so shortsighted. We can't just keep taking. The Earth already gives us so much, everything we need. We hope by the middle of the century, our economies will truly be based on sustainability and respect for all life."

"What are you most afraid of?"

Franny is afraid Canada won't ever formally recognize environmental rights. "Then we'll never have the legal tools to protect the people, animals, and places you love."

"I'm afraid humans will damage the Earth beyond repair," says Rupert.

"What do you worry about for your children's future?"

Franny's worry is that her children's generation won't get the chance to experience wild places. "They won't have access to clean air, clean water, and healthy food. They'll never be able to walk in an old growth forest or watch a salmon run."

Rupert's worry? "I'll have to apologize to my children about the state of the world they're inheriting, like so many adults are apologizing to me right now. I can see and feel their regret, their sadness."

"How hopeful are you that we can turn things around before it's too late?"

Franny is very hopeful. "People can't keep ignoring how we're impacting the planet. We are connected with the Earth. Whatever harm we do to our water, air, and land will come back to harm us. At some point, people will take action to turn things around, when they're personally at risk."

Rupert, too, remains hopeful. "Given the chance, the Earth will heal itself. We just need to get out of the way and begin to help this process."

"Do you believe we need a revolutionary change to society to avoid environmental disaster?"

Absolutely, believes Franny. "My mum says some people don't like the word 'radical'—but I do. Our life-giving planet doesn't need *little* changes. It needs *big*, radical, visionary changes. We can't lose any more irreplaceable species or damage any more ecosystems."

Another big "yes" from Rupert. "We need a revolutionary change in behavior and perspective. We need to change how we look at the planet as a resource, and how we always look at the economy and environment separately. We need to focus less on consumerism and more on adding meaning and respect to life."

Serious stuff.

But these two aren't all serious.

Franny enjoys finding ways to merge her love of the arts with her activism. "I spend lots of time reading, writing stories and poetry, drawing, and doing fabric art. I also love exploring long, obscure words or just reading the dictionary. One of my biggest non-advocacy goals is to publish a novel."

"I'm already looking forward to reading it!" I say.

Rupert wants to bring more music into his advocacy and more advocacy into his music. He wants to become an innovator in biotechnology, grow a beard, and get his driver's license—to drive an electric car, of course. "I've always loved music, food, and having a good laugh. I spend a lot of time

learning about history, reading sci-fi novels, playing and recording music, hanging out with my family and friends. My biggest non-advocacy goal is to be in a band. I also want to be happy and discover the meaning of life."

Throughout our interview, Franny and Rupert often veer back to gratitude—for the natural landscapes and supportive adults all around them. "We have been so lucky to be surrounded by adults who respect what we have to say, who understand our still-growing skills and knowledge, who have gone out of their way to help empower us, but still allow us to just be kids. Can you imagine what would happen if all young people were given the same support and encouragement to make change?"

Rupert and Franny believe that, regardless of the people and places that shape one's life, "all youth have the capacity and responsibility to make positive change in their families, schools, communities, and world. We want all youth to feel empowered and hopeful."

Most importantly, they say, kids should never let age get in the way of their dreams for a better world. "We agree that our biggest accomplishment was taking that first step into the world of advocacy. When we look back, we see it took a lot of courage for a seven- and a ten-year-old to take such a leap."

When it comes to environmental activism, Rupert and Franny are living proof that there's no minimum age required.

"There are so many people around the world who are doing amazing work to help people, animals, and the planet," says Franny. "They give me hope and they motivate me to keep doing my part. Also, my own environmental work motivates me. The more I do, the more I am inspired to keep going."

TRAILBLAZER TIPS

Be bold

One of our favorite quotes is: "Be bold and mighty forces will come to your aid." These words make us feel courageous when we're trying something we have never done, starting a new project, meeting someone new, or doing something scary. Be bold . . . take the first step . . . then another . . . then lots more.

Be a leader

Leadership means stepping up. Leadership means taking action. Leadership means inspiring and supporting others to do their best work. Leadership is believing in yourself and following your heart.

Find a mentor

Find someone who believes in you and can lead you along the way. Mentors and role models not only help you reach your goals, but they can also help you grow into your best self.

Ask for help

When you're young, you often don't have all the skills or experience you need to achieve your goals. Work hard, enjoy your successes, but be humble enough to ask for help when needed.

Find a balance

Beware of spending all your spare time doing environmental projects. Take time to nurture your other interests and passions. This in turn will give you more energy for your environmental work.

Start small, think big

We started with small actions but as our experience, skills, and confidence grew, we were capable of doing more.

Keep it personal

We try to connect with individuals. We try to treat everyone like a friend. We want youth to feel like they matter and they have something important to say and contribute.

Help others find their unique path

It's important to give youth time to integrate information. Don't tell them what to do or what to think or how to feel. Share information, then let them find their own path, their own voice.

Rupert (L) and Franny (center) hit the surf with their dad near Tofino, B.C.

A committed woman who has bridged the ice age to the digital age. Her sophisticated views on the environment and the way the world works are brilliant and convincing.

– Adrienne Clarkson, Former Governor General of Canada

Offers a perspective grounded in the culture and wisdom of northern people to preserve the "right to be cold."

– Lloyd Axworthy, Former federal Minister of Foreign Affairs

Sheila Watt-Cloutier is a true hero. She has stayed calm, controlled, and modulated for decades now as she has led the fight against pollutants and against climate change—led the fight for her Inuit brothers and sisters across the far north.

– Bill McKibben, Environmentalist, author

SHEILA WATT-CLOUTIER

....

Champion of Inuit Culture

Protecting the Arctic, saving the world

Home: Kuujjuaq, Nunavik, Québec
Pursuits: Inuit leader, environmental & cultural rights
advocate, author, and educator

After a friendly two-hour tea together months earlier, straight-talking, globe-trotting Sheila Watt-Cloutier was back in my hometown of Yellowknife and had granted me another chunk of her precious time for an interview. I chose to meet at our local library's Writer's Room, since, after all, we were both writers, and I liked the softly lit atmosphere in that tiny room, which, I learned, was about as big as Sheila's first house in Kuujjuaq.

I geared up for our interview by re-reading her best-selling book, The Right to Be Cold. *There, I read this line: "It has been my intention with every talk I give to compel citizens to act and bring about change." I suspected she saw this interview as an opportunity to do just that—to change the way I look at the Arctic world and its "brilliant culture," which she is doing everything in her power to protect.*

QAMUTIIKS AND AQPIKS

"The world I was born into has changed forever . . ."

So begins the account of a remarkable life in Sheila Watt-Cloutier's autobiography, *The Right to Be Cold—One Woman's Story of Protecting Her Culture, the Arctic, and the Whole Planet.* "Most shockingly, like all my fellow Inuit, I have seen what seemed permanent begin to melt away. The Arctic ice and snow, the frozen terrain that Inuit life has depended on for millennia, is now diminishing in front of our eyes."

The melting Arctic

The havoc unleashed by climate change is just the latest tidal wave of outside forces that have rocked Sheila's culture and environment. These profound changes are mirrored in the arc of her life, beginning one dark winter night in 1953 in Kuujjuaq, a tiny coastal town in Nunavik, Northern Québec.

As climate activist Bill McKibben says in the foreword to her book: "Sheila Watt-Cloutier is just old enough to remember what might be called the old Arctic."

With this in mind, I ask Sheila to take me back as far as she can, to a time when the basic fabric of her ancient culture was still intact—as was the cold.

"My earliest memories are traveling by dog team with my family to go hunting and ice-fishing. I would be snuggled into warm blankets and fur in a box tied safely on top of the *qamutiik*, the dogsled. I would view the vast expanses of Arctic sky and feel the crunching of the snow and the ice below me as our dogs carried us safely across the frozen land.

"My family was my mother, my grandmother, my two brothers, and my sister. In those days, most families lived in outpost camps outside of the community in *igluvijait* or igloos in the winter, and tents in the summer. We stayed a little closer to town because I was raised by single women."

This unusual family make-up could have been a big challenge for Sheila, growing up in a traditional culture where most people "lived by the ways of snow and ice" and depended on an elder male hunter for food. Luckily, her mother Daisy and grandmother Jeannie—the "Watt women"—were amazingly resourceful, both on the land and in the community, serving as inspiring role models for Sheila.

"My family lived very traditionally, eating what we call 'country food,' hunting, and fishing. We traveled only by dog

Living "by the ways of snow and ice" on a traditional Inuit qamutiik

team. My mother and grandmother taught me traditional women's skills, like working with animals to prepare food and clothing. My brothers always led the dog teams. At the end of each day, we would have remarkable food to eat together. We spoke nothing but Inuktitut during those first ten years. When in town, we lived in a little house that had no electricity, no running water."

"That your mother built, right?" I ask.

"Absolutely. My mother, as a single woman, with the help of my oldest brother, was able to build our home. She was ahead of her time, for sure. Very capable, strong, and dignified. We knew that it was rare for Inuit to build their own homes, much less an Inuk woman. It spoke to my mother's feistiness and confidence. She was determined to live independently in her own house. It was sort of matchbox-size but it was cozy. It became a place of security, comfort, and peace. So that's my humble beginnings."

"You write that your mother had a fiercely independent spirit. Do you think that rubbed off on you?"

"Oh, yes, there's no doubt. It comes out in the way I live and work and think independently. I'll always voice what I feel needs to be voiced, no matter what you think, as long as I know it's true. That comes from my mother. My brother says I can be very stubborn, just like her."

"I usually ask others in this book, 'How did your interest in nature begin?' But in your case, Sheila, you were literally *born* into it!"

Sheila laughs. "As Inuit you *are* born into nature because you're out there constantly. Nature fed and taught us every day. Everything was about the pursuit of food *in* nature. And so, nature meant everything to us.

➤ Sheila, her mother (L), and an auntie (with her hand in the bucket) take a break while out berry-picking.

"We had to know if the weather was good enough to travel, the condition of the ice and snow, if the animals were close enough. And it wasn't only about eating animals, but also using their by-products, especially furs. We'd always be sewing and preparing furs to make boots or coats or whatever was needed to stay warm out there. Everything we did every day was about the animals. The land, the water, all of nature was our supermarket."

"You describe in your book how hunting is so important in shaping character in young people, cultivating good qualities like patience and boldness and tenacity. Do you see that in your own growth?"

"Certainly that was true during the first ten years of my life, where nature and culture taught me directly. But I also witnessed their teachings in the hunters around me. For example, watching my brothers prepare the dog sled for the hunt, how meticulous and focused they had to be, to make sure everything was in the right place. All that took incredible patience to get ready for long trips to hunt caribou or go fishing.

"I learned the same way from my mother and grandmother—by observation. Especially how to prepare food from the land—what we call country food. This work demanded that we stay focused and patient to prepare things that literally kept us alive. Those lessons have never left me."

"It sounds like hunting was absolutely critical to your education and character development as a child. How do you talk about this with southern audiences who might have problems with a hunting-based culture?"

"I try to get people to understand that a way of life based on harvesting animals is not a confirmation of death but an affirmation of life. It's about life giving life. I teach that to children who have been conditioned to think the blood associated with harvesting animals is somehow awful or bad.

I teach that it is, in fact, a natural and wonderful thing when life gives life.

"When an animal is harvested with respect, gratitude, and connection, there is this remarkable bond when I have its blood on my hands. It is very much like gardens in the south when you have soil on your hands. Whether blood from an animal or soil from the Earth, it's all the source of life. It's all one.

"That's the picture I share—that it can be a very beautiful and joyful experience to be a hunter and really appreciate the food nature gives us. As a child, I absorbed that joy countless times. Ultimately, I learned that it was not just about feeding your body, but also feeding your soul. That is *so* important.

"Those things that touched me in my youth still connect me with my mother, my grandmother, my sister, and my aunts, all of whom have since passed away. Because we shared those experiences—harvesting, preparing, and sharing country food together—now, whenever I have my hands in animal blood, I find myself profoundly grieving their loss. But I also feel deeply connected to them because those experiences connected all of us to each other, to our culture, to nature, and to the animals that feed us physically and spiritually.

"And so, country foods remain a central part of where I've come from, who I am, and what I cherish."

"Besides hunting and preparing country foods, what were other favorite activities you enjoyed as a kid?"

"Our family hunting and fishing trips were an important part of my early childhood, but they represented only a fraction of the time I spent outdoors. For the children of Kuujjuaq, the great northern landscape was our playground.

In the summer, we explored the natural world, picking berries, looking for birds' nests, and playing on the hillsides surrounding our town. In the winter, we would sometimes slide down those same hills on sealskins."

➤ *"The great northern landscape was our playground."*

"What kind of berries would you pick?"

"It starts off with the *aqpiks,* or cloudberries, then blueberries, blackberries, and arctic cranberries. Like hunting, it's the connection to each other that was the best part—and still is today when I do it. We're not just out there picking berries. We're talking, visiting, taking a break with tea and bannock. Every scoop of berries brings you back to that connection with the land, with each other, and with spirit. It literally grounds you and helps clear your head of all kinds of silly nonsense. That's very special. And so, berry picking has always been sacred to me. It's an amazing experience for Inuit women and children to share together.

"It's those sorts of *connections* that I remember most from my days as a kid. Growing up in a boundless landscape and a close-knit culture is a kind of magic. Those early experiences on the land shaped me completely, until I was sent away at the age of ten."

DISCONNECT

Sheila spent her first decade of life grounded in a safe and sheltered world, where "everything mattered and everything was connected," where her life was "bonded with the ice and snow." But then the outside world did its best to unplug all those connections, one by one.

At age ten, Sheila's formal education was about to take a soul-wrenching turn, beginning with a quiet, well-meaning announcement from her mother. "After I finished my fourth year at school," Sheila writes in her autobiography, "my mother took me aside to tell me that my friend Lizzie and I had been chosen to go south to attend school. I didn't realize it at the time, but we were part of a federal government

➤ *Sheila (in front) and friends about the time they were uprooted from their Arctic home and shipped south to school*

program that selected 'promising' Inuit children with a potential for leadership to be educated outside of the Arctic."

The plan was to ship Sheila and Lizzie to Nova Scotia to live in the home of a *qallunaat*—or non-Inuit—family that had lived in northern Québec for many years. Her mother had worked for them as a cook and later as a medical translator for patients that only spoke Inuktitut.

"Although I really had no idea what all this meant, I was excited at the prospect of a new adventure. I wasn't at all worried about joining this *qallunaat* family and going to school so far from home. I was only ten, after all, and naïve about what it really meant to be away from my grandmother and community. I was in for a brutal shock."

The shock began on the plane ride south.

"The journey south was traumatic, foretelling of the struggles soon to come. I quickly became extremely motion sick on the long flight—so ill, in fact, that I had to put on an oxygen mask." After finally arriving in the lonesome coastal village of Blanche, Nova Scotia, Sheila was bedridden in the home of Joseph and Peggy Ross for three days, unable to eat. But the cloud of sickness that followed her all the way from Kuujjuaq was nothing compared to the heartache of being separated from her mother, grandmother, and community.

The next shock came with the food Sheila was forced to eat. The traditional country foods that she had grown up with and so loved, were clearly not on the menu—*muttaq* (whale blubber), seal stew, caribou meat, and arctic char. This proved to be especially hard for Sheila, since country food was "a powerful part of feeling at home." She found a lot of the southern food she was served, including fresh peas and milk, "revolting." In all the time Sheila spent in Nova Scotia, the closest thing to country food she and Lizzie ate was after they snared a rabbit and Mrs. Ross made them a rabbit pizza.

Then there were the clothing rules. Determined to hasten their adaptation to southern ways, the Rosses always put "prim and proper" dresses before comfortable sweaters or, God forbid, jeans.

*Isolated farmhouse near Blanche, Nova Scotia—
"like another planet" to Sheila*

As alien as the Nova Scotia landscape seemed to Sheila and Lizzie—basically like another planet—they occasionally stole an hour or two to explore the spruce woods behind the Rosses' house. But most of their free time was filled with chores around the house and farm, or sitting at a desk doing homework.

During Sheila's second year in Nova Scotia, she experienced one of the worst losses of her life—the death of her beloved grandmother, the primary mentor and unshakeable rock of her life. "My grandmother had always been so much more than a grandmother to me. She was my other parent. She was my foundation. My grandmother gave me command of my culture, my language, my food, my Inuk identity. I had spent all my early years at her side. She raised me. And yet, I don't remember crying at the news of her death. There were no loving and understanding arms to fall into for support."

Tormented by strange routines and restrictions, a gnawing tension in the house, and a lack of open warmth and affection, Sheila became desperately homesick. "We cried for two weeks non-stop. We wrote letters home telling our families that we wanted to return. Lizzie would send letters to her sister, Annie, most of the pages filled with, 'I want to go home. I want to go home. I want to go home.'"

One day, after the girls wrote a bunch of letters home and asked the Rosses to mail them, they came back from school to find the same letters spread out on the dining room table. "They had obviously been read. Even though I was very young, I felt my privacy had been grossly violated. But the experience got even worse. The Rosses told us that we were never to write letters home unless they had screened them first. In essence, we could not freely communicate how we felt to our families."

Even though Sheila grants her *qallunaat* hosts honorable intentions—not wanting her real family to worry—she writes that, "the effects of this censorship were profound. In one simple act, the Rosses helped to weaken my voice for years to come."

As crushing as the Rosses' rigid rules may have been, they did help Sheila excel at school. She quickly mastered the English language, often out-performing her Nova Scotia-born classmates. "To this day, I still have the silver dollar that I received for being at the top of the class."

But her academic winnings came at a steep cost—the withering away of her Inuit knowledge, skills, and connections. During those two years, she lost a remarkable amount of her mother tongue. "I remember trying to practice Inuktitut before heading home for the summers so I wouldn't feel so lost with my family and community. But it proved to be surprisingly challenging, and sometimes embarrassing."

Another crushing blow to Sheila's voice and self-identity.

Whenever she returned to her community, she was painfully reminded of how much she was missing. "During the years we would spend away from home, other girls our age were learning how to prepare country food, embroider, and sew. They were mastering the cultural skills of working with caribou hide, sealskin, and goose down."

Not Sheila and Lizzie. The door to that kind of schooling slammed shut the day they boarded the plane to fly south.

MINISKIRTS AND BASKETBALLS

During her second summer home from Nova Scotia, Sheila found enough of her voice to spill her unhappiness to her family and, later, the agent from the Department of Indian Affairs. "In those days, government officials had a lot of power, so it was hard not to feel frightened or distressed."

In the end, this high-powered *qallunaat* had a sympathetic ear and agreed not to send Sheila and Lizzie back to Nova Scotia. Instead, like thousands of Indigenous children across Canada, they were assigned to a residential school, the federal government's mighty assimilation tool for hammering southern values into northern kids.

That fall, Sheila and Lizzie stepped aboard another plane headed south. Destination: Churchill, Manitoba. At age twelve, Sheila would be the youngest student enrolled in the Churchill Vocational Centre. "But this time, we had the familial comfort of our sisters and the company of many other Inuit teenagers."

Though the presence of closely connected kids made Sheila feel "a whole lot safer," her first hours in this new institution came as a shock. "Remember, we were young children and teens, arriving in the middle of the night in a strange setting. The greeting party was a group of strangers who numbered our clothes, treated us as if we were infested with lice, and lined us up half-naked for showers. There was no dignity in this introduction to our new home, not to mention a blatant absence of welcoming, loving energy."

When I ask Sheila how she survived "that very oppressive system," I am surprised by her answer.

"Churchill was different from many of the residential schools you hear about. It was generally not as abusive. What helped me survive was a real sense of family among the 200 Inuit kids there. And they kept us busy from morning to night, especially with sports. I loved, loved, loved sports— basketball, volleyball, gymnastics—and became very good at them. I loved dance, too. That kept me really excited about life there.

"Most of the experiences from Churchill were fairly positive, even though we knew from the start we were going there to be re-programmed in many ways. But in general, we were safe there. We were together."

After three years in Churchill, Sheila was selected to attend high school in Ottawa, where she suffered another round of acute homesickness. Yearning for the comfort of her fellow Inuit, and tossed about from the chaos of frequent moves—four families in three years—Sheila struggled in school like never before. As her grades sank, so did her confidence, forcing her to abandon her dream of becoming Nunavik's first doctor.

"After spending eight years in southern Canada, raised by strangers, going to school far away from home, being disconnected from family, culture, traditions, and community, and losing so much of those formative developmental years, at eighteen I decided it was time to go home."

Free at last to choose her own path, Sheila followed the magnetic pull of her inner compass. It pointed north, back to the Arctic.

> "*In a real sense, Inuit of my generation have lived in both the ice age and the space age. The modern world arrived slowly in some places in the world, and quickly in others. But in the Arctic, it appeared in a single generation.*"

Sheila's home town of Kuujuaq today

HEALING AND HELPING

Back in Kuujjuaq, Sheila discovered a community "battered and bruised" by government-imposed policies to modernize and assimilate Inuit culture. Alcoholism and violence were on the rise, along with a kind of hopeless despair.

The RCMP's slaughter of sled dogs across the Eastern Arctic—over twelve hundred in all—was just one among many traumas that had deeply wounded Sheila's community while she was away at school. Done supposedly to prevent an epidemic of canine distemper and attacks by sick dogs, they were often gunned down in front of their owners. Sheila tells the story of how, during the height of the slaughter, her uncle Johnny received a knock on his door, only to have an officer "throw his new harness in his face and tell him, without remorse or apology, that he had just shot his dogs."

So much pain, horror, and change. It was almost too much for eighteen-year-old Sheila.

"As a teenager, I didn't really understand the root of these problems. Having been sent away and then come back and seen all the changes, I went, Wow! There's more fear in the community now. Less safety.

"Seeing my mother helping the community, I knew from a very young age that I wanted to be of service to the communities. That was my driving force."

So, at eighteen, soon after returning from Ottawa, Sheila followed in her mother's footsteps, starting work as a medical translator at the town's tiny hospital. She admits this was a bit ironic as she had lost so much of her mother tongue. But, in spite of occasional bloopers and embarrassment, she persevered, eventually regaining her fluency—her *voice*. "I felt elated with my growing comfort with Inuktitut and loved this work that connected me with the entire community."

It also let her give what she could to the healing of her people. "I was at the frontline of the traumas and the injuries, the abuses, and the violence. All these problems just skyrocketed."

As Sheila gained experience in the health field, and later as an educator and mother, she came to see that a lot of the escalating issues in her community had roots—and solutions—in the outside world. She realized the need to join the dots among problems related to health, culture, and environment. These issues can't be "siloed," she insists, but must be understood and tackled as a whole.

There goes Sheila again, making connections.

These insights, and her growing profile in the wider Inuit world, led her to take the leap into Indigenous politics.

"From my own memory, I've seen the Inuit collectively move from a remarkably safe, secure culture that taught our children how to meet the opportunities and challenges of life, to this traumatized place of fear and fragility. How did that happen? In one lifetime?"

"In your lifetime," I say.

"Yes, in *my* lifetime. So, I moved into the international arena. I wanted to learn more about these issues on a global scale and help protect a way of life that we had lost so quickly."

Soon after Sheila was elected as the Canadian President of the Inuit Circumpolar Conference, or ICC, another trauma emerged: persistent organic pollutants, so-called POPs. These included DDT and other agricultural chemicals, that leap-frog in the wind, up from the warm south, then condense and fall to Earth in the cold northern air, accumulating in the precious fish and wildlife that Inuit love to eat.

"Wow! What kind of world have we created?" Sheila asks me. "When Inuit women had to think twice about nursing their babies with toxins found in our country foods. That's when my sense of helping really came into play. As an elected international leader, I made it my mandate to protect us from being poisoned from afar."

"How did you bring your own cultural lessons into your new job?"

"I drew on the skills of the Inuit hunter spirit I'd learned as a child—to remain patient, calm, reflective, focused, and centered. Those traits served me well in leading the global campaign against POPs." Sheila's calm and controlled approach to international negotiation helped put a human face on an issue, which, till then, had been just an environmental problem. The result was the 2001 Stockholm Convention on Persistent Organic Pollutants, and a multinational ban on the development and use of POPs.

In a real sense, that fight was Sheila's training ground for an even larger, ongoing battle against global climate change.

> "My homeland—the Arctic—is the health barometer of the planet. What is happening today in the Arctic is the future of the rest of the world."

The Arctic: our planet's "health barometer"

THE HUMAN FACE OF CLIMATE CHANGE

You've heard the dire warnings. Disaster is right around the corner. Climate experts claim that a global temperature increase of just two degrees will push human civilization over the brink.

How soon?

Pretty soon, when you figure that humans release about 400,000 Hiroshima bombs' worth of heat into the atmosphere every day.

So, where's ground zero?

That's an easy one for Sheila. She'll point to the land of ice and snow where she grew up. She knows first-hand that the Arctic is warming way faster than anywhere else on Earth, already logging an average temperature rise almost *twice* the supposed tipping point of two degrees. In fact, Sheila's homeland, so long defined by cold, is now warming faster than the experts ever predicted.

It's no surprise that Sheila has no time for scientists, politicians, and TV talk show hosts who like to debate whether climate change is real or not, and, if it is, just when exactly we can expect catastrophic climate change to come knocking at our doors. For Sheila and her Arctic world, the climate catastrophe is real and it's now. The disaster has already begun.

"We're not preparing for it, we're *living through it*, and it's getting worse."

What's happening up there?

Sheila will tell you that what's happening is not just about starving polar bears and "other fuzzy animals we like to love." And it's more than the shrinking sea ice, collapsing coastlines, wonky weather, and melting glaciers that we read about in headline news from the far north. For Sheila, what's most important—and so often forgotten—is how all these changes impact the *people* of the Arctic in truly devastating ways, threatening their lives, culture, and property.

And so, Sheila talks about the Arctic as the "early warning system" for the state of our planet's climate. She calls her fellow Inuit—and Indigenous people around the world—the "global sentinels of climate change," since they live so close to the land. "The land, that is such an important part of our spirit, our culture, and our physical and economic well-being, is becoming an unpredictable and dangerous place for us. Our wisdom, which comes from a hunting culture dependent on ice and snow, is as threatened as the ice itself."

That's the bad news Sheila hammers home to audiences around the world.

And the good news—what she calls her personal mantra?

"By protecting the Arctic, you save the planet."

I ask Sheila to unpack her mantra for me.

"The world grapples with questions like: What are the impacts of climate change? What does it really mean? How do we deal with it? How urgent is it? Well, I say look to the

Those aren't ants. They are Inuit people (and their snowmobiles, L) sending a warning to this warming world! The Inuktitut word below the drummer says: LISTEN.

people that directly rely on the climate and their environment to survive on a daily basis. There is so much the whole world can learn from the Inuit and the Indigenous world."

"Could you say the same about small island nations that are disappearing into the sea—save those islands and you save the world?"

"Perhaps. But those islands are going underwater *because* the Arctic is melting and the sea level is rising. You can't find a clearer example of that physical connection with the Arctic— of how it plays a huge role in global impacts. The Arctic is the starting point of all of these changes."

The power behind Sheila's message comes not only from her own life story, but also from another multinational study she worked on that combined the world's best scientific and traditional knowledge on Arctic climate impacts. "Before this study, it was always about ice or polar bears. You rarely saw the human dimension to this issue."

Sheila spreads her message:
"There is so much the whole world can learn from the Inuit."

Sheila gave the human face of climate change an even higher global profile by launching an international legal challenge, claiming that its impacts "violated Inuit rights to practice and enjoy their culture." Sheila's unique view of climate change through the lens of human rights led to her nomination for a Nobel Peace Prize.

"You've been named a 'Champion of the Earth,'" I say, as our precious time together ticks down. "What would you call yourself?"

"Never an *activist*. I am not a person to protest and go screaming in the streets. I call myself an environmental, cultural, and human rights *advocate*. I call the talks I give teaching moments, so in that sense, I still call myself a teacher."

"Well, I've certainly learned from you, Sheila. Thank you. Any closing message?"

"My main message is that the Inuit culture is a powerful, brilliant, and wise culture, and can teach the world a thing

➤ *Making connections: Swedish climate activist, Greta Thunberg, clutches a copy of Sheila's book,* The Right to Be Cold.

or two about long-term sustainability. For me, the bottom line is, if we can solve the Indigenous crisis, including Inuit of the Arctic, we solve the global climate crisis. If we solve the climate crisis, we solve the economic crisis. I see those as intimately connected."

I give Sheila a lift to her hotel on the other side of Yellowknife. As we part, I ask her to sign my copy of *The Right to Be Cold*. Before driving off, I peek at what she's written.

"Good to meet and connect."

"Climate change is about people as much as it is about the Earth, and the science, economics, and politics of our changing climate must always have a human face."

TRAILBLAZER TIPS
....

Learn from Indigenous cultures

Learn how the deep connection Indigenous cultures still have with the natural environment gives them a unique view on the impacts of climate change and possible solutions for the wider world.

Get out on the land

In our swirling, hurting, fast-changing world, it's all the more important to take time and get out on the land to reconnect yourself with what's real, what's important, and what's possible.

Find the human face

Like Arctic climate change, there is a human face behind most environmental issues. Don't bog down in strictly physical or scientific details. Look to the people most impacted for solutions.

Don't "silo" issues

Issues related to health, culture, or environment can't be "siloed" or looked at in isolation if we want to rise above them. They should be understood and tackled as an interconnected whole.

Tell people what you're for

I have always engaged in the politics of influence rather than the politics of protest. I will march for something but not against. Act in ways that bring people together, not split them apart.

Find your voice

Don't let any institution or politics unfairly restrict your thoughts, words, or actions. Find your independent voice and use it freely to express what you feel is true and needs to be voiced.

Lead from love, not fear

When faced with seemingly impossible obstacles, don't give up. Beware of the paralyzing power of fear. Find strength in the long-term value of your work and the loving connections it builds.

Don't "other one another"

When it comes to climate change, it's too easy to "other one another" and think it's somebody else's problem. Whether living in the north or south, it's a shared challenge for us all to work on.

Learn what you can give

I never tell young people exactly what to do. It's different for everyone, yet we all have something to offer. Learn what you can give. Your own wisdom will kick in and the right action will follow.

"An amazing odyssey . . . A record of sheer courage, stamina, and stubbornness."

— David Suzuki on *Being Caribou*

"Heuer is a man with a great imagination and an even greater dream.

— Don Starkell, author of *Paddle to the Amazon*

KARSTEN HEUER

···

Epic Adventurer

Protecting wildlife, one mind-blowing journey at a time

Home: Canmore, Alberta
Pursuits: Wildlife biologist, park warden,
author, and explorer

The spring sun is barely tickling the tops of the limestone peaks above Karsten Heuer's log-sided home in Canmore, Alberta, when he greets me at his front door. Before settling in for our interview around his cozy dining table, he offers me a strong cup of black tea—which I welcome, given that it's 6:00 AM and I've just driven all the way from Calgary, over an hour away.

Karsten had texted me the day before, proposing a breakfast meeting. After months of tracking him down like an elusive mountain lion—he's one busy biologist—I instantly texted back, "Sure." I'd envisioned a casual mid-morning conversation in some funky Canmore coffee shop. Then came his next text: "How about my place, 6:00 AM?" I blinked hard and replied, "Perfect!"

I greedily slurp my tea and, before I can hit "record" on my voice recorder, Karsten's wife and partner in conservation, Leanne, pops out, waves "Hi" and ducks out the door for an early morning run.

I start by suggesting to Karsten that, "You're one of Canada's best storytellers, so you know the value of a good story."

Karsten laughs. "I'm not sure many people would agree with you, except maybe my boss. 'Oh, there's Karsten, one of his stories again!'"

After serving up several cups of tea and a perfect spinach-cheese omelette, Karsten leaves my head swirling with his stories of incredible journeys on backcountry trails.

THE SEED

The boy was already soaked and shivering within two minutes of leaving the van. Who in their right mind would be marching to Dog Lake in Kootenay National Park in late fall, by flashlight, up a steep mountain trail, in the middle of a sleet storm? Well, Karsten Heuer and his dad, that's who.

Karsten pulled up his collar and did his best to match his father's snappy pace. He knew there was no turning back. That's not how it worked.

How it worked was this: Leave Calgary at 3:00 AM, sleep in the back of the Volkswagen van the whole way to the mountains, get to the trailhead at 5:00 AM, hike another hour in the dark to a pristine alpine lake, and get a worm on your hook by the first sliver of dawn light—the best time for trout to bite. By the time Karsten was eleven, he had got this routine down cold.

But, as the dark, dripping pair hurried through the deserted Dog Lake campground in the freezing drizzle, their well-oiled routine was shattered by a blinding light.

"FREEZE!" shouted a voice out of nowhere as a huge floodlight stopped Karsten and his dad in their tracks. A uniformed man stepped out of an outhouse into the light and grilled them about what exactly they were doing there at this odd hour.

"The guy worked for parks?" I ask Karsten, forty years later.

"Yup. A national parks warden. He'd sat in that outhouse all night, in the rain, waiting for potential poachers to fall into his trap. He let us go once we came clean.

"I remember walking away completely dumbstruck, thinking, 'Like, wow! Jobs like this actually *exist*?' I was full of admiration for the passion and commitment this guy had shown that dark, wet night, all to protect wildlife. Looking back, I think that experience was definitely a seed for me."

"Did you ever meet the guy again?" I ask.

Karsten laughs. "To this day, I don't know who it was. It would be kind of fun to shake his hand!"

> "*T*hose early mornings—birds singing, mist rising off the lake, the vanilla scent of pines hanging in the air— really stick in my mind. Whenever I see, hear, or smell those things now, I feel like I've returned home."

PICKLES OF TROUBLE
....

Karsten was born to German immigrant parents within sight of the Rocky Mountains. He thanks his mom and dad for his lifelong love of nature. "That was a big driving force for them to immigrate to Canada—to be out in wild places that Germany couldn't offer. They were pretty fanatical. Every Friday night they'd pack up the van and off we'd go to hike, camp, fish, or cross-country ski in the mountains."

➤ *Karsten as a baby on his mom's back during one of his first hikes into the mountains*

After the crazy outhouse hold-up on the Dog Lake trail, Karsten's parents recognized his sudden obsession with park wardens and gave him a copy of *Men for the Mountains*, by Alberta's celebrated poet-warden, Sid Marty. That book, much of it written by candlelight in remote mountain cabins late at night, was perfect fertilizer for the seed that had taken root in young Karsten.

"*Men for the Mountains* was a window into a way of life

*Karsten (far right) with his family at a backcountry lake
after an early morning hike to go fishing*

and a job that was all around me but, till then, had been kind of invisible."

Besides eating up mountain adventures—whether on the trail or in books—Karsten loved to bike to Weaselhead Flats, an amazingly wild area beside Calgary's Glenmore Reservoir. He and his buddies would spend all day fishing and exploring, with Chloe, his salt-and-pepper Terri-Poo, bounding ahead. "We sometimes ran into black bears. We caught absolutely massive rainbow trout. We had a lot of freedom. It was pretty sweet.

"All this happened within bikeable distance from home, but it was still a big deal to get there. And sometimes we got ourselves into little pickles of trouble. Everything kind of goes wrong, but we always got ourselves out."

"Pickles of trouble," I say. "I love that. Any stories?"

"Like snagging your favorite fishing lure and, instead of tugging till you break the line, all of a sudden one of us peels off his clothes, jumps in, and gets swept downstream because he didn't account for the current, and brushes up against a log jam.

"Or like when we caught these eight-pound trout and didn't have a bag or anything to take them home for dinner. So, we had to ride one-handed with these big fish over our shoulders, right down 37th Street, and all these cars honking at us."

"What about your dog?"

"I'd trained Chloe to ride with me on the bike. So there I was, with this little Terri-Poo around my neck like a fur shawl, and a big fish over my shoulder. She caught the attention of a newspaper photographer and we appeared the next morning on the front page of the *Calgary Herald*."

Karsten (right) with a friend and his dog, Chloe, who liked to wrap around Karsten's neck while he tore down the street on his bike

Even as a kid, Karsten felt a strong sense that "something was missing" in the landscape where he grew up: bison.

GOLDEN GOAL

Even during those carefree days with his fishing buddies, Karsten worried about the big changes he saw in Canada's fastest growing city. "Calgary grew *so* much through my childhood. Things were completely transformed. The ditches and fields where we played were literally filled and paved over for roads right in my neighborhood."

Outside of town, what upset Karsten was what he *didn't* see. "All those weekend trips from Calgary, driving through the prairies to the mountains, I remember feeling a strong sense that something was missing. Bison. I can't put my finger on how I knew this. Really, I think books had a huge role. I'd read lots of stories about those vast herds of bison that once crossed the landscape where I grew up."

Karsten's early stirrings that something was wrong in the natural world, and that maybe he could do something about it, prompted him to set his sights on what he called his "golden goal"—to become a park warden.

"Even in high school, I knew that a university degree alone was not going to cut it. I realized that, if I really wanted to be a warden, the other part of the equation was to get some field experience. So, I sought out volunteer opportunities."

Karsten's father was not thrilled with the idea of his son working for free. "He would have been happier, quite frankly, if one of my jobs in high school was stocking shelves in the local Safeway. Or if I became a full-time grocery clerk. He figured I was nuts. He honestly thought I was being taken advantage of. He didn't see the big picture. But my mum did, and she was encouraging.

"For me it was worth more to keep my long-term goal in mind, to actually contribute to something I cared about. I was learning to listen to my own heart."

WAKE-UP CALL

Karsten's trust in himself paid off, big time, when he scored a volunteer job tracking radio-collared wolves in the wild mountain heart of Kananaskis Country, west of Calgary. Wolves were returning to this area for the first time in years and no one knew where they came from, how they moved, or how they survived. It was a ground-breaking study. And there's Karsten, out on a mountain trail again, slowly spinning a hand-held antenna to catch signals from a pack of wild animals he could actually help protect. "It was pretty helpful to have this kid down there who would phone in the location of these wolves. If I hadn't volunteered, nobody else would've, and it wouldn't have gotten done."

More than discovering the excitement of field work, Karsten was discovering a whole new world. "I remember seeing my first wolf. This animal, that had only been a mythical creature, all of a sudden was *real*. That was a big wake-up call. The whole place came alive in a different way because now there was this silent, hidden world going on in the background that you're not even aware of unless you've experienced it. That was a much larger reward than any paycheck you could put in the bank."

One volunteer job led to another, and soon Karsten was tracking coyotes in the wilds of Banff National Park, thanks to some of the wardens he'd got to know through his wolf work. But not all the jobs he hunted down were as fascinating or fun. Like the long days he spent doing autopsies on road-killed elk in an old cattle barn, where the floor was seething in maggots. "That definitely was a grunt job!" says Karsten, laughing.

It was a slow progression toward his golden goal. Karsten continued volunteering for wildlife work well into his university years. He still worked for free, but those jobs allowed him to experience in real life things that had only been stories on the pages of his favorite book, *Men for the Mountains*.

MAKING A DIFFERENCE

Karsten finally got a foot in the wardens' door halfway through his biology studies, when Parks Canada hired him as a summer student. Soon after he graduated, a promotion fell into his lap. Introducing: Karsten Heuer, seasonal warden at Banff National Park! The job he'd dreamed of for half a lifetime.

"Being seasonal gave me time to experiment with other things like photography and writing—skills that became important later in life." It also allowed Karsten to explore some really cool wildlife projects, working at the feet of Dr. Cliff White, a top-notch biologist who became a lifelong mentor. "Cliff had this amazing ability to stretch you, to give you jobs that were just on the edge of your abilities. Looking back, you might think, 'Why didn't he look for someone more experienced?' But he could see your potential, and he'd always provide opportunities to grow."

Now, here's Karsten, in his early 20s, at the very beginning of his career as a wildlife biologist, and the first study Cliff hands him is to figure out what exactly it is about the town of Banff that blocks the movements of animals. Long before such questions were on anyone's radar, Cliff recognized the importance of wildlife corridors—or "habitat highways"—to protect healthy animal populations. He knew that mountain towns like Banff can squeeze out the natural flow of animals like a deadly blood clot in an artery. But he didn't know how.

Cliff turned to Karsten for answers.

"It was a real growth opportunity, for sure," says Karsten. Starting from scratch, he had to design a whole new study, hire a crew, then spend weeks in the field, trying to figure out what the heck was going on. By closely tracking the movements of wolves, cougars, wolverine, and lynx, Karsten eventually identified the exact pinch points blocking the flow of wildlife traffic around Banff—human stuff like roads, rails, airstrips, and horse barns.

"This compelling story began to emerge. Things began to line up. We started going public with our results and got lots of support."

➤ *Karsten has been radio-tracking coyotes, wolves, grizzlies and other wild animals since he was a teenager.*

Karsten drew up a bunch of recommendations that basically blew open the entire wildlife corridor. Much to his surprise, all of them were carried out within a few months. The results were stunning. The next winter, Karsten's team detected a 700% increase in wolf traffic. "For my first big project, that was really empowering. I was, like, 'Wow, you really can make a difference. You can change things!'"

"I've matured, but the thing that really motivates and energizes me—working directly with animals—that hasn't changed since my teenage years."

Karsten triumphantly raises the Y2Y flag after scaling yet another mountain pass.

YELLOWSTONE TO YUKON

This success story, plus a radio-collared wolf named Pluie (French for "rain") that crisscrossed an unbelievable chunk of the Rocky Mountains, inspired a project that would put Karsten on the world stage of wildlife conservation. It was called "Yellowstone to Yukon," or Y2Y, a visionary idea to connect and protect key wildlife corridors along the spine of the Rockies from Yellowstone National Park way down in Wyoming, to Canada's Yukon Territory, 3,400 kilometers away.

To make this vision a reality, a joint Canada-U.S. organization was set up to get any groups with an interest in this vast mountain landscape talking to each other about how best to protect wildlife—conservation groups, scientists, First Nations, businesses, landowners, and governments, big and small.

Not an easy job when everybody craves a piece of the landscape pie.

Working in Banff National Park, Karsten knew well what a challenge this would be. Just getting such diverse and often conflicting groups in the same room, let alone agreeing on anything, seemed like an impossible dream. Besides, who the heck had ever heard of Y2Y?

Karsten figured the Y2Y vision could use a little pumped-up publicity. He decided to *walk the whole thing*, doing community presentations and grabbing media attention along the way, to share his adventures and talk up the vision. He would see for himself what wildlife barriers did or did not exist, from start to finish.

"Y2Y was such a great idea that I needed to tell others, and do it in as compelling a way as possible. I decided to try and *be* one of those grizzly bears, wolves, or wolverines, making the whole journey, walking, step-by-step, from Yellowstone to Yukon."

Granted an extended leave from his park warden job, Karsten picked up his 80-pound pack—about half his body weight—and took his first steps north from Mammoth Hot Springs in Yellowstone National Park on June 6, 1998. Where trails existed, he hoped for a walking speed of four kilometers an hour. He halved that for steep ascents, bushwhacking, and trail-making, which were basically the norm for much of his epic journey. "It was all guesswork."

Yellowstone to **Yukon**
Conservation Initiative

Karsten's 188-day trip equaled traveling from Canada to Mexico and halfway back again. As for climbing, he calculated that the 107 passes he crossed were like he'd climbed Mount Everest twenty times.

Like I say, epic.

En route, he survived several nail-biting encounters with grizzly bears, black bears, avalanches, monster storms, river crossings, even death threats from angry opponents of the Y2Y vision—loggers, miners, or ranchers who saw the Y2Y conservation vision as a menace to their bread and butter.

➤ Karsten inspects grizzly digs on his 188-day Y2Y hike.

In the end, Karsten feels it was worth the sometimes "Olympian" effort and life-threatening risks. He'd raised the Y2Y flag through more than 200 public presentations in towns along the way, done hundreds of newspaper, magazine, radio, and TV interviews, and made "wildlife corridor" a household word throughout the huge region he'd hiked.

Among the greatest "blessings" of the trip, Karsten points to the person who joined him for some of the toughest

Karsten, Leanne, and Webster follow grizzly trails over a remote mountain pass in the Rockies.

sections of the journey, Leanne Allison. "I came to realize she would make a pretty good wife. We got married soon after the trip was over and have been soul and trip mates ever since."

Karsten shared their journey in his best-selling book, *Walking the Big Wild—From Yellowstone to Yukon on the Grizzly Trail*. Since then, Karsten's name and the Y2Y vision have been virtually synonymous. "I'll be a lifelong ambassador," he says.

NECESSARY JOURNEYS

Karsten's Y2Y hike turned out to be just the first of several epic journeys—what he and Leanne call "necessary journeys"—done for the cause of wildlife conservation.

Leanne silently joins the flow of caribou traffic across the Arctic tundra.

"By the time we'd finished the Y2Y hike, we knew we had a pretty good model for telling a conservation story to a lot of people. We decided to do it again, only this time, we wouldn't just symbolically walk where the animals might travel. We'd try and follow 120,000 caribou on foot, in real time." That story is told in his second book, *Being Caribou*, which follows their five-month trek across the "frozen" Arctic, alongside the Porcupine caribou, as they migrated from the Yukon mountains to their super-sensitive calving grounds along the northern coast of Alaska. The journey itself and, later, the award-winning book, went a long way to raise public awareness of the dangers of oil drilling on the herd's calving grounds.

Karsten and Leanne hatched another mega trip in 2007, this time joined by their two-year-old toddler, Zev, and the family dog, Willow. The goal: to walk, paddle, and sail from their home in Canmore to Cape Breton to meet Canadian

literary legend, Farley Mowat, another passionate conserva-
tionist, writer, and mutual fan.

The family carved a path across the prairies, tundra, forests,
and coastlines by stringing together cool places featured
in some of Mowat's stories. "We wanted to give the stories
time to speak to us as we passed through those landscapes."
True to style, they arranged public presentations along the
way and released a sweet movie about their five-month,
5,000-kilometer trip called *Finding Farley*.

"It's funny," reflects Karsten. "People think, 'Oh, you want
to do this epic trip!' But honestly, on all our trips, it was more
about the *story* we wanted to tell than the trip itself. We never
dwelled too much on the question, 'Is this trip even possible?'
It was more like, 'How are we going to get people's attention
for these animals and landscapes that need protection?' And
then it was, 'Oh, maybe if we hike it, that would bring the
story alive.' Whether it was physically possible became a
minor detail. We knew we could figure out a way."

L to R: Claire Mowat, Karsten, Farley Mowat, Leanne and son Zev

Karsten's story comes full circle with his latest pet project—returning bison to Banff National Park after an absence of almost 150 years. "You know, it's funny to connect the dots backward. Here I am, trying to reintroduce plains bison, the largest land mammal in North America, back to the very landscape where I felt that absence as a kid."

As for future projects, Karsten and Leanne have a big idea up their sleeves but aren't yet ready to go public. You can bet, whatever it is, they will be journeying together, with boots or skis or paddles, intimately connected to the Earth.

And it will be epic.

> "*When I look at the map, I'm amazed at how far I've come. But day by day, it doesn't seem a big deal. I think that's what excites me most. It shows what's possible when one chips away at something.*"

HOPE FOR WILDNESS

Did Karsten rely on superhero talents, courage, or strength to pull off his incredible journeys? "Heck, no," he'll tell you. Instead, he credits his success to the colorful threads that spun his boyhood dreams.

Like hiking with his dad up a dark mountain trail, by flashlight, in sleet storms, with bears all around. Or catching monster trout with his fishing buddies at Calgary's Weaselhead Flats. Or, as a teen volunteer, tracking wolves and coyotes across the jaw-dropping mountain country in and around Banff National Park.

"When you go out on an adventure, whether it's a few hours in a natural area in Calgary, or it's months in the Yukon wilds, there's a sense of accomplishment, of self-confidence, that grows in you. Also, that special joy and peace that comes from being in nature. I felt all those things really early in my life. And today—probably till I die—I naturally gravitate to those places for the same feelings and rewards they offered me as a boy. Those childhood experiences were quite normal for me and taught me to feel at home in wild places that 99% of people might think were scary."

Karsten also credits his success to the "gift" of where he grew up. Those wild and shining mountains that shaped his dreams keep on giving, steering his work, fueling his optimism for the future.

"We live in a place of hope. Things are still possible here that aren't in other parts of the world. You see the inspiration on the faces of visitors who come to see wildlife. That's why I really glommed onto the bison project. I see it as something hopeful, an antidote to the despair that a lot of people feel. It's an opportunity to show people there's still hope for wildness, even here, not far from a city of 1.3 million people."

Karsten tells me this as I drive him to work, from Canmore to Banff, zooming down the Trans-Canada Highway, which is entirely fenced off to protect animals, except for special wildlife bridges and underpasses that Karsten helped design.

"You know, it is kind of miraculous," he says. "Here we are, driving 100 kilometers an hour on a six-lane highway. Our national railway is just through the trees beside us. You drove here this morning from Calgary, just an hour away. And yet, there's probably a grizzly within a kilometer of us right now, maybe a family of them. That's because of a lot of local success stories that help us co-exist with wild animals."

Karsten's conservation work promotes peaceful coexistence between wildlife and us.

As if on cue, Karsten spots a small herd of bull elk grazing on a sunny slope protected from the highway.

"Look at this!" he shouts with an unspoiled boyish wonder. "I've been seeing these guys every morning on the way to work. Pretty amazing!"

Karsten guides me to the Banff National Park warden office, gives me a quick tour inside, slips on his green warden's jacket, then heads into the field to check on his bison. Reaching for the door, I pause in front of an old black-and-white photo of wardens sporting wide-brimmed hats and seasoned smiles that speak of many adventures in the wild.

Karsten and Leanne on Day 150 of their epic trek following the caribou

True men for the mountains.

I lean into the photo, looking for the mysterious warden in the outhouse who spooked young Karsten that dark, rainy night, over forty years ago, and set him on a path that led to this very door.

> **"I** can still go back to the Dog Lake trail and it's unchanged. It's the same trees, the same shoreline, the same beaver lodge. There's something pretty comforting about that.**"**

TRAILBLAZER TIPS
....

Stay positive

Dwelling on the darkness, the bad news, the negative—this will paralyze you. Instead, focus on the light, the good stuff, the positive, and things will open up.

Trust in yourself

Listen to your own heart. Obey your inner compass. That's the most important thing. Listen to that and act on it.

Do what you love

It's good to recognize what makes you tick, what energizes and motivates you. Know your talents, skills, and passions and use them to wedge open those cracks of light.

Focus

I tend to be pretty focused. There are a lot of issues in this world. Have confidence in others working on those issues. Otherwise you can spread yourself too thin and get scattered.

Beware of naysayers

Naysayers will tell you all these reasons why not to do things. Weigh what they say but don't let them blind you. Find the fortitude to push a little further, to sometimes swim upstream.

Keep hope alive

If you're in despair, it shows you're aware enough to see problems. The trick is not to throw up your hands but to harness that awareness. Make it your motivation. Move toward hope, not despair.

Tell a story

Use storytelling to change public sentiment and to pressure decision-makers to move toward the kinds of goals you want to achieve. A compelling story can really bring an issue alive.

"We still work with giants in our midst. For me, one of those giants is the remarkable landscape architect Cornelia Hahn Oberlander . . . Cornelia's landscapes are legendary."

– Sandy James, City planner

"Oberlander is a trailblazer for women and for landscape architecture, always addressing the distinct cultures and landscapes of Canada, where she is now a national treasure."

– Kenneth Helphand, Landscape architect

"Oberlander is one of the greatest landscape architects of the modern era . . . At the age of 96, she is still an unstoppable force of nature, working on several projects and doing advocacy work."

– Hadani Ditmars, Journalist

CORNELIA HAHN OBERLANDER

Green City Pioneer

Bringing nature to cities for over 70 years

Home: Vancouver, British Columbia
Pursuits: Landscape architect

As I dial Cornelia's phone number, I swipe a film of sweat off my brow. I'm feeling a tad intimidated, about to interview Canada's "Queen of Green." I already know that she hates it when writers "don't get it quite right" when telling her story. I also know that, at 97, she's still busier than I may ever be.

Who am I to waste this woman's precious time?

Finally, after many rings, I hear, "Hello?" in a clear, no-nonsense voice with a lilting Germanic accent.

"Hello, Cornelia. It's Jamie in Yellowknife."

"Yes. So what would you like to talk about?"

"First, I want to thank you for agreeing to be a part of this book for young people and—"

"I have very, very little time for things like that. You heard that from my daughter?"

"Yes, I did, so, ah, maybe I'll get right to it . . ."

It gets better.

Though I'm still sweating, I eventually earn Cornelia's trust as we share stories about a building we both love very much.

TOUCHDOWN

For over fifteen years, I had the fun of being the Monday morning nature guy on CBC North radio. Always recorded in the wild, I would invite listeners outside, from across the Northwest Territories, to witness the return of spring birds, explore a beaver lodge, or dissect a snowbank. Absolutely anything to do with the natural world was fair game for my audio adventures.

So, one frigid February morning in 2005, I decided to do a piece on my second favorite building in the whole world (the first being my house). That would be the Legislative Assembly, the NWT government's hub of supreme power neatly parked in the boreal woods beside Frame Lake, a snowball's throw from downtown Yellowknife.

Honestly, the place looks as if a massive flying saucer had dropped from the Arctic sky and touched down in those woods, without toppling a tree or squashing a squirrel. Having landed on my piece of the planet, it belongs there as much as the two-billion-year-old volcanic rock lining the lakeshore.

You can tell I'm jazzed about the place from this radio snippet. "I walk around this lake at least once a week and,

Northwest Territories Legislative Assembly—a giant spaceship nestled in the boreal forest

every time I look at this place, I just want to get down on my knees or jump in the air or clap my hands. It's just so beautifully integrated with nature—its location, its shape, its colors, the landscaping . . ."

The landscaping.

Who designed the landing pad for this environmentally sensitive spaceship? None other than the *grande dame* of landscape architecture, Cornelia Hahn Oberlander. Before this craft fell to Earth in 1993, Cornelia was tromping through the woods and bogs with her clipboard and shovel in hand, reading the land. She took notes on the tallest trees—which really aren't very tall up north—and the tiniest mosses and lichens. She got down on all fours and examined the scanty soil and ancient rock. She studied the play of sunlight and shadow through the willows.

A vision took shape in Cornelia's mind: to preserve the rugged yet delicate beauty of the site by seamlessly stitching the assembly building into the wild woods and lakeshore. She would do this by using only local plants that grow naturally in the area.

Under Cornelia's direction, the access road was re-routed around a super-sensitive peat bog. To repair any damage to the bog, she devised a "cookie tray technique" that turned earthmovers into giant spatulas to skim off slabs of peat and graft them onto the wounds. She ordered that all trees within eight feet (2.5 m) of the building be saved during construction. Woe betide any worker who broke her rule—they were either fined or fired. She collected local seeds, cuttings, and tissue cultures, propagated them in a Vancouver greenhouse, then shipped more than ten thousand plants back north for planting around the construction site.

In the end, you won't find any blazing garden beds, no flowering trees, no juniper hedges carved like lions or dinosaurs. Cornelia's painstaking work at the Legislative Assembly is basically invisible. Any normal human being couldn't tell she'd done anything at all. She actually calls this technique "invisible mending," a term she borrowed from sewing, where landscapes around buildings are restored in such an extraordinary way, they look like they've been there forever.

The damage inflicted by building the "Ledge," as we locals call it, was invisible by the time the parade of politicians and their staff moved in. To pull this off in a frigid climate, where it might take a hundred years to grow a ten-foot tall tree, was almost miraculous.

Some trees inevitably had been flagged for removal to make way for the 46,000-square-foot building. Just before the bulldozers started rolling, some buddies and I rescued several pickup-truck loads of spindly birch and spruce trees. We delivered them to my backyard, where I planted my own forest, now thick enough to hide my whole house.

"I'm sorry I missed you in Yellowknife many years ago," I tell Cornelia. "I'm really impressed with your sensitivity to the land, how you can, as you say, 'read the site' so carefully."

"I taught myself all this. All my projects deal with ecology."

"I thought you'd be interested to know that I saved a lot of trees from that property."

"From the peat bog?"

"Yes."

"Good. Frame Lake, so beautiful. I love it."

Of the many green projects Cornelia has worked on around the world—from a living roof on top of the Canadian embassy in Berlin, to a mossy, birch-lined courtyard inside the *New York Times* building—the NWT Legislative Assembly in my home town of Yellowknife remains, to this day, one of her favorites.

Cornelia's success at so beautifully stitching the Ledge into a virgin northern landscape is a shining example of her creative genius for working *with* nature, not *against* it. It protects a precious green space near a busy downtown core; it heals the land after major construction; and it invites people to enjoy a sweet synergy between the natural and built environment.

This flagship project, carried out in the wilds of northern Canada, embodies the fulfillment of a dream that took root in young Cornelia's heart over ninety years earlier in a simple garden half a world away.

> *"Landscape architecture is growing a piece of what is there. The site must speak. I must find the spirit of the place. What it is that gives the place its character."*

A DREAM IS BORN
....

Born on the summer solstice, June 20, 1921, Cornelia grew up in the industrial heartland of Germany along the Ruhr River valley. "My mother, being a horticulturist, didn't like it there. The coal dust hung everywhere. So we moved further south to a village near Dusseldorf. We had a beautiful garden where I always amused myself. These are my very first memories."

Cornelia's mother readies her young daughter for a special outing.

Cornelia had her very own vegetable garden when she was just four years old. "My mother introduced me to all the plants. She would ask, what would you like to grow? I planted peas and corn. So, very early, I knew the joy of growing. There was also a forest, where I found wonderful anemone flowers, which I still have in my garden today."

By the time Cornelia was eleven years old, she had an even bigger garden behind her new home in Berlin. One

From a very young age, Cornelia knew the joy of flowers,
forests and gardens.

day her mother decided to take her to an artist's studio to have her portrait done. Cornelia would much rather have puttered in her garden, ridden her horse, King, climbed trees, or gone swimming in a nearby lake, but her mother wouldn't budge. Getting a portrait done for every girl before their twelfth birthday was a strict family tradition that went back generations.

So, there sat Cornelia, in the artist's hot, stuffy studio, doing her best not to wiggle. Occasionally, when the artist looked down at her paints, Cornelia would steal a glance at a curious mural on the wall. She learned it was a map of the Rhine River, flowing through an imaginary town, jam-packed with brown roads and red houses. "When I asked the artist about the green spaces in this mural, she told me these were parks. When I got home, I asked my mother about the plan, and she said it was done by a landscape architect. I wanted to make parks so, on that day, I decided this would be my profession. I knew this from my eleventh year onwards."

Repelled perhaps by memories of coal dust and factories around her first home in the Ruhr valley, eleven-year-old Cornelia saw the lack of green spaces in cities as a big problem. From that pivotal day in the artist's studio, she made up her mind to fix that, eventually becoming a global force in the green city movement.

At age eleven, I had all sorts of grand plans about what I'd be when I grew up—from fireman to forest ranger, astronomer to astronaut. None of those dreams panned out because I didn't have the hard-nosed determination and focus that Cornelia did at that age.

You might think she came by this naturally when you look at her family background. Her mother was more than your average garden-variety horticulturalist. She pioneered the introduction of new kinds of crop seeds into Germany and authored several gardening books for children—while raising and home-schooling her own. Cornelia's Uncle Kurt founded the internationally famous outdoor survival school we know today as Outward Bound, as well as United World Colleges, a global education movement that brings together high-school students from all over the world to learn, most importantly, about each other.

A lover of parks, 11-year old Cornelia decided that she would make them the focus of her life's work.

Whatever endowed Cornelia with all that *chutzpah*—an unbreakable will to get something done—she would soon discover many roadblocks that stood in the way of realizing her dream, not the least of which was a man named Adolph Hitler.

ESCAPE

Cornelia spent more and more time tending her garden, learning from her expert mother how to care for different plants, soils, and pest-eating birds and insects. But even as she put down deeper roots behind their home in the leafy suburbs of Berlin, her parents, Franz and Beate Hahn, were making careful plans to uproot and escape to America.

The problem: Cornelia was born into a Jewish family caught in the deadly clutch of Nazism.

Adolph Hitler's rise to power had been fueled by a promise to rebuild Germany's economy after its crippling collapse following the First World War. By the early 1930s, Hitler had convinced many Germans that Jews were to blame for all the country's problems and vowed to do whatever it took to get rid of them.

On New Year's Eve, 1932, Cornelia's father and mother raised a glass and secretly promised each other to leave Germany, and soon. But just twelve days later, Franz, while doing what he loved best, skiing in the Swiss Alps, was swallowed whole by an avalanche.

"So, Mother was left with three children, Hitler, and no husband."

In spite of this tragedy, Beate Hahn held firm to her promise to leave Germany. She adopted a "life must go on" attitude for her three daughters, supporting their English and French lessons, arranging musical events, even organizing ski trips, an activity that remained a family favorite.

By the time Cornelia entered high school, she was the only Jewish girl in her class, because so many of her friends' families had managed to escape.

Her mother was determined to join the exodus of German Jews, but the window of opportunity was closing fast. The sound of "Heil Hitler!" rang in the streets. The sky over Berlin lit up night after night from burning books viewed as anti-government, including all Jewish books. Jewish children were banned from attending school. News of random arrests and disappearances spread among the Jewish community.

Then, one Sunday in 1935, Nazi officers pounded on Cornelia's door. Wearing shiny black boots and uniforms emblazoned with swastikas, they pushed into the dining room where the family was eating. They demanded to inspect the house for any items now forbidden to Jews, including banned books or roast beef, searching for any excuse to arrest them all.

Fourteen-year-old Cornelia was terrified, unable to believe what was happening. They had done nothing wrong. In her mind, they were hardly even Jewish. Yes, they celebrated Hanukkah, but they also had a Christmas tree.

Once the soldiers had stomped through the entire house and found nothing, Cornelia's mother politely asked them to leave.

The tipping point for Beate Hahn—and for many Jews still trapped in Germany—came on November 9, 1938. It became known as *Kristallnacht*, the "Night of Broken Glass," when the Nazis went on a rampage, destroying Jewish homes and businesses across Berlin. In the end, they burned 191 synagogues and arrested 20,000 Jews.

Luckily, Cornelia's home was spared, but Beate knew that, at any moment, the Nazi soldiers could return to their door and drag them away.

Two weeks after *Kristallnacht*, Cornelia, her mother, and two sisters joined the 40,000 Jews fleeing Germany that year. Grabbing only one small suitcase each, they set Beate's carefully laid plan in motion: on the way to the train station they'd stop at a hotel to pick up Sir Alexander Lawrence, a British friend of Cornelia's Uncle Kurt (remember the Outward Bound guy?), take a train to Belgium, a ferry to England, and the *Queen Mary* to New York.

Destroyed synagogue after Kristallnacht

All went according to plan until they hit the German border.

"Mrs. Hahn, get out!" yelled a Nazi soldier who stormed into their train compartment.

Cornelia held her breath.

Lawrence sprang out of his seat and announced he was accompanying this lady and saw no reason why she should get out. He then engaged the soldier in polite conversation about how impressed he was with the lawfulness of German society. He managed to keep him talking until their train car lurched forward. Caught off guard, the soldier had to jump through a window as the train pulled out of the station, carrying Cornelia closer to freedom, and her dream.

Years later, Cornelia asked her mother how she coped with the rising violence against Jews during those chaotic years. "I envisioned a path," Beate replied, "a long, straight path with posts on either side. At the end was our new home. I just kept following that path, never straying from it."

Sound familiar?

Like mother, like daughter.

THE PATH OPENS

On February 23, 1939, Cornelia got her first glimpse of New York Harbor from the towering deck of the *Queen Mary*, the world's second-largest passenger ship. At seventeen, she wanted nothing more than to blend in with other American teenagers in their saddle shoes, bobby socks, and short hair. She told her mother that her German braids had to go.

After sampling the town life of New Rochelle, in lower New York state, Cornelia's mother felt that New York was "too materialistic" for her girls. And, once again, she longed for a bigger garden. So, she went out and bought a whole farm, a safe distance away in New Hampshire.

There Cornelia spent her first year in North America, helping her mother seed crops, husk beans, and manage the farm. Some mornings, when her "firecracker daughter" was getting underfoot, her mother would send Cornelia into town with a truckload of vegetables to sell at a local market. "I learned organic gardening years before I became a landscape architect."

When the snow came and the farm work slowed, Cornelia threw herself into her favorite pastime, skiing.

As much as Cornelia enjoyed farm life, after a few months, it could not contain the dream burning ever hotter in her chest—to find a college that could teach her the art and science of landscape architecture. Then, "lo and behold," as Cornelia says, while poring over a thick college catalogue, she discovered Smith College in neighboring Massachusetts. It offered a landscape architecture program aimed exclusively at women in a field generally hogged by men.

Cornelia immediately filled out a college application, then waited anxiously for a response. And waited . . . and waited some more.

At first, Smith College was reluctant to accept her, maybe because of her German background. But when she sent them her high school average of 96%, they gave her a firm thumbs-up. Within a year of arriving in the United States, Cornelia was enrolled in the program of her dreams.

It was love at first sight.

Arriving on campus, she was struck by the huge oaks and speckled plane trees, the lush botanical gardens, the arboretum full of plants from around the world. "What I loved most was the placement of the buildings around the pond." They called it Paradise Pond, and this was indeed a kind of paradise for Cornelia.

Besides being a perfect place to learn her chosen craft, Smith College offered Cornelia a buzzing social scene to learn how to be American, another of her top priorities.

You can feel her struggle to fit in from an English essay she wrote while still a teenager. "There are long periods where I don't think of being a foreigner. But then again, a sudden little incident might shake me, throw me back . . . It happens sometimes when I go to a house of a friend. I often have to tell of our escape. I am made to feel like a movie and I don't feel real: I suddenly notice that there is a high wall between me and my hosts, which neither of us can cross." Her essay ends with a bold commitment to "discard sentiments, look into the future," and "understand the demands of America."

Cornelia's dorm room was right across the hall from that of Betty Friedan, editor of the school newspaper and a hard-core feminist, who would later write the earth-shaking bestseller, *The Feminine Mystique*. Friedan often hosted long, loud discussions in her room about everything from fascism to feminism, much to the annoyance of hard-working Cornelia. One night around 2:00 AM, during a particularly rowdy discussion on the fate of female graduates, Cornelia leapt out of bed, flung open Friedan's door and yelled, "If you are worried about working or not working, just get a profession and get to work!" Then she slammed the door behind her.

Cornelia immersed in a garden during her college days

Cornelia found the learning a thrill, finally set loose to unlock the secrets of landscape architecture. How to creatively use earth, rock, water, and plants like a landscape painter uses paints. How to weave things like fences, pathways, and gazebos into a pleasing landscape package. How to plan green spaces, not just for private homes, but for larger public buildings, even whole cities.

But not all of Cornelia's classes thrilled her. She found an early morning botany class especially challenging, not because of the hour, or the subject matter, but a supremely uninspiring professor. One morning, she had to throw her clothes over her PJs to make it to class. Another day, she rushed in without breakfast and snitched a plateful of fruit intended for class dissection. For this minor misdemeanor, the professor sentenced her to a four-week suspension.

Undeterred by one grouchy prof, Cornelia put her head down and excelled in botany, and all her other courses, finishing a four-year program in just three years.

And still she hungered to learn.

So, what next for what one journalist called, "this crazy girl who wanted to design modern landscapes?"

To Cornelia, the choice was obvious: Harvard University. She knew it offered one of the world's best graduate programs in landscape architecture.

But wait. Remember, landscape architecture was largely a man's world back then. Harvard only admitted men to this program.

Serious roadblock.

But it's 1942. The U.S. is at war overseas. Many young men had signed up to fight and Harvard's enrolment was nosediving. So the school fathers buckled and reluctantly agreed to admit women—but only "for the duration of the war."

Cornelia's timing couldn't have been better. On March 5, 1942, she got the "We are pleased to inform you . . ." letter from Harvard's Graduate School of Design. That summer, she joined the second class in the school's long history to include women.

Cornelia took to Harvard like a duck to water. There she built on the foundation she'd laid at Smith College, learning how to read the ecological nuances of a site, make detailed landscape plans, and build terraces, walls, and pools. She was learning, as she says, "the art and science of the possible."

By this stage of her studies, Cornelia had developed a fondness for modern design. So it's no wonder that she knocked heads with a certain professor who was stuck in another era. When he asked his students to draw a "service entrance" on their house plans, Cornelia politely told him that not everyone could afford servants. When he asked them to adopt designs used by dead kings and noblemen, Cornelia chose to use forms that "modern people could understand." When he asked his students to use loose watercolor paints in their plans, Cornelia instead used crisp stenciled lettering and sharply inked lines.

Clearly, Cornelia was charting her own course when she graduated with a Master's degree in landscape architecture in 1947. This was quite a feat, given that most of her female classmates, enrolled in a school that had made special arrangements to include them, abandoned their studies as soon as World War II ended, to go home, get married, and raise babies.

HOLDING TO THE DREAM

Over the next twenty years, Cornelia did all that, too, but never abandoned her dream. By the time the 1960's rolled around, Cornelia had married her grad school sweetheart, Peter Oberlander, moved to Vancouver, and become very good at juggling wifely and motherly demands with her blossoming career.

"In three and a half years, I had three children. What could I do? I did playgrounds." These were not ordinary playgrounds, with teeter-totters and swings bolted to the ground. Cornelia created hills and valleys, tunnels and treehouses, woods and water. Her playground designs reflected her growing environmental belief that, "if kids don't have contact with nature, how will they ever understand and care for it?" As for her own kids, she would often combine *her* work and *their* play by taking them along to the construction site. "They didn't notice what mother was doing."

*Shepherding her lively young family in 1963,
while never abandoning her dream*

Cornelia became known as "that play lady," building seventy playgrounds across the country. In Canada's centennial year, 1967, she built her most famous playground at Montreal's Expo 67. During the six-month fair, 30,000 children from over 60 countries played there.

When I ask Cornelia what she feels is her biggest accomplishment, it's not her world-famous Expo playground, or the National Gallery in Ottawa, or the Canadian Embassy in Berlin. It's Robson Square in the heart of downtown Vancouver.

On top of this three-block-long office complex, Cornelia created a fantastic living roof from over 50,000 plants, arrayed to express the natural environments of British Columbia. Go sit in this magnificent green oasis, complete with towering trees, waterfalls, fountains, and cool shady nooks, and you'll find it hard to believe you're on the roof of a major downtown building.

➤ *Cornelia revolutionized playgrounds by offering kids a variety of adventurous activities, like at Expo 67.*

"I did lots of research to find plants that could withstand urban pollution and could be used on a roof. I researched everything—finding a lightweight growing medium, water-proofing the building, preventing root penetration, irrigation, everything."

Arthur Erickson, the world-renowned architect who hired Cornelia for this job, had nothing but praise for her problem-solving wizardry. "One of the most remarkable things about Cornelia," Erickson told a journalist, "is her ability to find a solution to difficult challenges through research."

Built in the late 1970's, Robson Square became a model for green roof design in North America, and Cornelia went on to literally write the book on how to build them.

Cornelia feels this project was a major turning point in her career, one that gives life to her vision of fully integrating landscapes and buildings in ways that are not only artistic and people-friendly, but also ecologically sound. "It's not just so the building and the land around it look good together. It is a matter of our planet's survival."

*Robson Square—a magnificent rooftop oasis
in downtown Vancouver*

> **"T**oday more than ever, with population pressures and green spaces getting gobbled up, people will need more places to reconnect with nature within cities.**"**

DOING IT HER WAY

As much as the world embraced Cornelia's innovative ideas, roadblocks still sprang up in front of her, sometimes due simply to her gender. "All I could think of was going out there and making the world a little greener. I never looked right or left. That's the only way I could succeed in this man's world."

Even after practicing as a professional landscape architect for over sixty years, she still finds she has to convince some clients that she knows very well what she's talking about. And, as something of a rebel, she often finds bureaucratic red tape a huge frustration. "It stops you every five minutes. If you have innovative ideas, then you have to constantly invent ways and means, with research and examples, to convince people who aren't ready for change."

Still succeeding "in this man's world"

"Where do you find the energy or inspiration to do your work?" I ask her.

"I get energy by taking care of myself. Eating healthy food, getting exercise, getting sleep, and spending time with my friends and family. I get my inspiration from the site itself and from my own research. Students also inspire me. I was over at UBC last week to listen to some presentations, and I am thrilled to know there is a new generation of landscape architects afoot that understands nature, ecology, and climate change."

Even as she approaches 100, this woman of attitude is still hard at work, greening our cities. I ask what's keeping her busy these days.

"I'm working on a habitat wall for birds and bees. It's an office building in east Vancouver. We are looking for an ornithologist who can tell us what birds will need to nest there."

"Fascinating."

➤ *Closely supervising a work crew at Vancouver's VanDusen Botanical Garden*

"And now I have to deal with the Vancouver library. We are behind schedule because the contractor threw out some of my grasses and he doesn't know where to get them. So, I'm scrambling on real jobs."

"Do you still get out in the field with your shovel?"

"Yes, I *do*!"

Cornelia was spotted just a few winters ago, with gum boots to her knees, standing in the middle of a winding, pebble-lined pond she designed beside UBC's Museum of Anthropology. Taking pictures for a Christmas card? Nope. Actually, she was conducting a personal inspection of the pond's filtration system.

And there's those birch trees in the *New York Times* courtyard that she designed years ago. Somebody goofed on the maintenance and now she's actively trying to replace the trees.

Then there's . . .

Well, you get the idea. Busy lady.

On top of her work, Cornelia gets regular requests for lectures, interviews, film and book projects. "After so many years, I am still astounded!" says her daughter Wendy, who works as Cornelia's right-hand woman. "At 97, there are just not enough hours in the day!"

"I'm very, very busy this week and next," Cornelia tells me, as I sense our interview abruptly winding down. "Then I have to go to Ottawa to become a Companion in the Order of Canada."

I learn that this award is given each year to only a handful of people who have "demonstrated the highest degree of merit to Canada and humanity." Think: Canada's Nobel Prize.

"There are lots of letters behind your name, Cornelia."

"Yes, and there will be many more next week!" she says, laughing. "I've been at this for a long time, Jamie."

Harking back to Cornelia's first garden in Germany, I make it 94 years and counting. She's been downhill skiing for almost as long, finally giving it up in her early 90s after a rogue snowboarder knocked her flat. But she remains a regular walker, swimmer, and cross-country skier, ever grateful for what she can do every day.

"The greatest satisfaction is to be creative," she told children's author Kathy Stinson in her brilliant biography of Cornelia, *Love Every Leaf*. "Every day I jump out of bed because I enjoy it. It's also tremendously satisfying to have people come, see what you've done, and go away wanting to do it for themselves."

That would be me.

Deeply moved by Cornelia's handiwork at Yellowknife's Legislative Assembly building, with its magical union of forest, rock, and water with concrete, steel and glass, I was inspired to engineer a forest of my own on the moon-like roadbed where I built my house. Years later, it looks like that forest and house have stood there, side by side, forever.

"Thank you, Cornelia, for taking the time to—"

"Yes, yes. You have to come here. I'll take you to some places. Okay?"

"I would love that. In the meantime, I promise to keep an eye on the Legislative Assembly for you."

"Good, good. All the best. I wish you well, but you still have a long way to go."

"Yes, I do."

"Every day, one step at a time."

"Good advice. Take care, Cornelia."

"And you, too. Nice to talk to you, Jamie. Goodbye."

"Goodbye."

My last words to Cornelia, whispered after she hangs up: "What a sweetheart!"

> *"I have never deviated from my dictum to bring nature into the city, and make people enjoy nature. And the passion is what drives me to keep going— just to make the world a little greener."*

TRAILBLAZER TIPS
....

Do your homework

To make the world greener, you need to do lots of research. Do your homework, bring your research to the table, and you will be better equipped to solve problems and convince people.

Take risks

Don't shirk from risks if you have new ideas that may be unwelcome by others. I was raised in the Outward Bound tradition, and there you learn to take risks and benefit from them.

Take back the green spaces

Enjoy and protect green spaces in the city that bring people, young and old, close to nature. Promote their therapeutic value for busy urban people who use only electronic devices.

Use the 5 P's of people management

These tips will help you deal with the inevitable "human factor" of any project:

- **Patience** – *People may need time to see things your way.*
- **Persistence** – *Stand up for what you feel is right.*
- **Politeness** – *Always treat people pleasantly, respectfully, and they'll more likely be convinced by your ideas.*
- **Passionate** – *Don't be afraid to share your passion. Others will be inspired.*
- **Professional** – *Regardless of differences of opinion, stay professional, not personal.*

Find your niche

Find your unique niche or specialty. Something you are passionate about. Then you will succeed in your chosen work. You cannot practice the whole gamut. Focus and find success.

Start small, think big

When you are extra busy, choose something manageable that you excel at. That will give you confidence to do bigger projects when you have more time to devote to them.

Involve kids

Find ways to involve young children in your projects. They have an instinct for environmental work and need to hear your message. They like hands-on, seeing, tasting, smelling, touching.

BLAZING YOUR OWN TRAIL

The early shaping forces that sculpted each of these exceptional lives are wildly different.

Sophia Mathur was born into two generations of climate activists.

Ian McAllister got slung in a basket over an environmental war zone.

Elizabeth May discovered that somebody poisoned her pet lambs.

Ethan Elliott said "yes" to an environmental youth camp.

Anne Innis Dagg visited giraffes at the Chicago Zoo at age 3.

Kathleen Martin loved to perch in treetops and write stories.

John Theberge had a friendly neighbor who showed him a swan.

Rupert & Franny Yakelashek showed up at a grassroots celebration with David Suzuki.

Sheila Watt-Cloutier traveled by dog team over the Arctic ice.

Karsten Heuer followed his dad into the mountains to go fishing.

Cornelia Hahn Oberlander spotted a curious mural on the wall of an artist's studio.

Dots joined over the arc of each of these lives, long or short, reveal a dozen completely different paths. Yet, scratch the surface of their trails and you find similar roots:

A dream for a better world.

A deep desire to realize that dream.

A willingness to work hard.

A belief in the power of one to make a difference.

And the knowledge that the power of two or more, working together on the same cause, far exceeds the sum of the parts.

Dig deeper still and you find common threads beneath their trails, like the silent, unseen network of fungi that connects and supports all trees:

Find your voice.

Trust in your wisdom.

Do what you love.

Do your homework.

Never give up.

Keep hope alive.

Embrace mentors.

Tell a story.

Capture the heart (and the hand will follow).

Celebrate victories.

Stay positive.

And, oh yes: get outside.

Sometimes it's tough to blaze our own trails, to mark a path for others to follow, especially in these darkish times. I wrote this book to make that job a little easier.

Still, sometimes you'll be out there in the thick of it, head down, bushwhacking, and you'll lose the trail completely.

You suddenly realize you're lost and alone.

You're getting scared.

You can feel hope dripping away from every pore.

You look up, feeling helpless, waiting for the sky to catch fire, for all the pretty birds and butterflies to fall to Earth.

Eco-apocalypse waits for you around the next corner and there's nothing you can do about it.

Stop.

Breathe.

Look carefully for the next blaze.

Listen for other footfalls, human or otherwise.

Trust that at least you're headed in the right direction.

And most importantly, never, ever forget that you are not alone.

Take inspiration from the words of epic hiker and fellow adventurer, Karsten Heuer, as he searches for a "ghost path," high in the misty mountains he loves so much and will do all he can to protect.

> *I realized that although trails are lost, they don't*
> *just disappear. Instead, they are ghost paths,*
> *small imperceptible threads hiding until a ridge,*
> *a shoreline—any edge favoured by animals—*
> *appears again, and enough of them gather to*
> *reform the fabric of a visible trail.*

DIGGING DEEPER

··

KEY REFERENCES, VIDEOS, AND WEBSITES

SOPHIA MATHUR – CLIMATE CHANGE CHAMPION

Intergovernmental Panel on Climate Change (IPCC):
ipcc.ch

Citizens' Climate Lobby (CCL) Canada:
canada.citizensclimatelobby.org

The Lancet Countdown – Tracking Progress on Health and
Climate Change: lancetcountdown.org (watch the video)

Greta Thunberg's TED Talk:
ted.com/speakers/greta_thunberg

TIME magazine's tributes to Greta Thunberg as a global
youth leader and 2019 "Person of the Year":
time.com/person-of-the-year-2019-greta-thunberg
time.com/-greta-thunberg-next-generation-leaders

IAN MCALLISTER – DEFENDER OF THE RAINFOREST

Pacific Wild: pacificwild.org

Great Bear Rainforest – the movie:
greatbearrainforestfilm.com

McAllister, I., and A. Van Tol. *Great Bear Rainforest: A Giant-Screen Adventure in the Land of the Spirit Bear.* 2019. Orca Book Publishers.

McAllister, I., and R. Kennedy, Jr. (Foreword). *Great Bear Wild: Dispatches from a Northern Rainforest.* 2014. Greystone Books.

McAllister, I., and N. Reid. *The Great Bear Sea: Exploring the Marine Life of a Pacific Paradise.* 2013. Orca Book Publishers.

McAllister, I., and N. Reid. *The Sea Wolves: Living Wild in the Great Bear Rainforest.* 2010. Orca Book Publishers.

McAllister, I., and N. Reid. *The Salmon Bears: Giants of the Great Bear Rainforest.* 2010. Orca Book Publishers.

McAllister, I., and K. McAllister. *The Great Bear Rainforest: Canada's Forgotten Coast.* 1997. Harbour Publishing.

ELIZABETH MAY – AN EXTRAORDINARY ACTIVIST

Elizabeth's webpage: elizabethmaymp.ca

Kickass Canadians biography: kickasscanadians.ca/elizabeth-may

May, E. *Who We Are: Reflections on My Life and Canada.* 2014. Greystone Books.

May, E. and Z. Caron. *Global Warming for Dummies.* 2008. Wiley & Sons Publishing.

May, E. *How to Save the World in Your Spare Time.* 2006. Key Porter Books.

ETHAN ELLIOTT – VOICE FOR YOUTH AND BEES

Bee City Canada: beecitycanada.org

Bee Schools across Canada:
beecitycanada.org/become-a-bee-school/current-bee-schools

Ontario Nature's Youth Summit:
ontarionature.org/events/youth-summit

ANNE INNIS DAGG – THE WOMAN WHO LOVES GIRAFFES

The Woman Who Loves Giraffes – the movie:
thewomanwholovesgiraffes.com

Anne's favorite giraffe conservation project in Kenya:
reticulatedgiraffeproject.net

Innis Dagg, A. *Smitten by Giraffe: My Life as a Citizen Scientist*. 2016. McGill-Queen's University Press.

Innis Dagg, A. *5 Giraffes*. 2016. Fitzhenry and Whiteside. (children's book)

Innis Dagg, A. *Giraffe: Biology, Behaviour and Conservation*. 2014. Cambridge University Press.

Innis Dagg, A. *Pursuing Giraffe: A 1950s Adventure*. 2006. Wilfrid Laurier University Press.

KATHLEEN MARTIN – SEA TURTLE SENTINEL

Canadian Sea Turtle Network: seaturtle.ca

Kathleen's blog posts: seaturtle.ca/blog

Appenzeller, T. "Ancient Mariner." *National Geographic*. May 2009. (also available online if you search this title and author)

Romano Young, K. *Sea Turtle Rescue: All About Sea Turtles and How to Save Them*. 2015. National Geographic Children's Books.

Martin, K. *Kamakwie: Finding Peace, Love and Injustice in Sierra Leone*. 2011. Red Deer Press.

Martin, K. *Sturdy Turtles*. 2000. First Avenue Editions (children's book)

JOHN THEBERGE – PROTECTING WOLVES AND WILDERNESS

Theberge, J., and M. Theberge. *The Ptarmigan's Dilemma: An Exploration into How Life Organizes and Supports Itself*. 2010. McClelland & Stewart.

Theberge, J., and M. Theberge. *Wolf Country: Eleven Years Tracking the Algonquin Wolves*. 2001. McClelland & Stewart.

Theberge, J. (editor). *Legacy: Natural History of Ontario*. 1989. McClelland & Stewart.

Theberge, J. *Wolves and Wilderness*. 1975. Dent Canada.

FRANNY & RUPERT YAKELASHEK – FIGHTING FOR GREEN RIGHTS

David Suzuki Foundation's Blue Dot campaign: bluedot.ca

David Suzuki's blog post about Rupert: bluedot.ca/stories/david-suzuki-growing-environmental-leadership

United Nations report *Children's Rights and the Environment*: https://www.unenvironment.org/resources/other-evaluation-reportsdocuments/childrens-rights-and-environment (then download pdf with this title)

SHEILA WATT-CLOUTIER – PROTECTOR OF INUIT CULTURE

Watt-Cloutier, S. *The Right to Be Cold: One Woman's Story of Protecting Her Culture, the Arctic and the Whole Planet.* 2016. Penguin Canada.

Impacts of a Warming Arctic – Arctic Climate Impact Assessment: amap.no/arctic-climate-impact-assessment-acia

Sheila's TED Talk: tedxyyc.ca/videos-2016/human-trauma-and-climate-trauma

KARSTEN HEUER – EPIC ADVENTURER

Karsten's "Necessary Journeys" webpage: beingcaribou.com

Being Caribou – the movie: nfb.ca/film/being_caribou

Finding Farley – the movie: nfb.ca/film/finding_farley

Yellowstone to Yukon Conservation Initiative (Y2Y): Y2Y.net

Heuer, K. *Being Caribou: Five Months on Foot with an Arctic Herd.* 2007. McClelland & Stewart.

Heuer, K. *Walking the Big Wild: From Yellowstone to Yukon on the Grizzly Bear's Trail.* 2002. McClelland & Stewart.

Marty, S. *Men for the Mountains.* 2000. McClelland & Stewart.

CORNELIA OBERLANDER – GREEN CITY PIONEER

Herrington, S. *Cornelia Hahn Oberlander: Making the Modern Landscape*. 2014. University of Virginia Press.

Stinson, K. *Love Every Leaf: The Life of Landscape Architect Cornelia Hahn Oberlander*. 2008. Tundra Books. (children's book)

Biography, photos & videos:
tclf.org/pioneer/cornelia-hahn-oberlander

MORE ENVIRONMENTAL LEADERS FROM AROUND THE WORLD

Canada's Top 25 Environmentalists Under 25:
thestarfish.ca/top25

The Green Interview by Silver Donald Cameron:
thegreeninterview.com

Acknowledgments

··

How do you thank someone who's saving the planet? The life stories in this book are my offerings of thanks to a dozen ordinary people doing extraordinary things to do just that.

I am grateful to all of them for rekindling my faith in "the power of one" to bring about positive change, for stoking my hope for the future, and for dispelling my fear that there's little we can do but grab a handrail and watch our planet go down the toilet.

That's not to say that this wasn't a scary project. For instance, how did I feel about knocking on doors or dialing up phone numbers to ask total strangers, "Could I please write the story of your life?"

That got me sweating.

Another hair-raising part of this book journey, even when working with those I already knew, was sending out my draft chapter on each of them, then holding my breath while they picked over *my* version of *their* lives. After all, this is pretty personal stuff!

In the end, my fears evaporated, replaced by gratitude and joy.

From start to finish, each and every person featured in this book gave me all the time, toil, and trust it took to get their story right, and to package it, complete with very personal photos, in a way that will inspire others to become fellow changemakers.

For everyone's commitment to this project, and their belief in me to pull it off, I am deeply and eternally grateful.

I must once again thank my tireless, occasionally ruthless, but always wise editor, Peter Carver, who, for the nth time in our 20-year partnership, helped me find the fire behind the smoke of my early drafts.

Many thanks also to Richard Dionne, Kong Njo, and the skilled crew at Red Deer Press for shepherding this book from initial brainstorms to final polishing and production.

Finally, a huge, heartfelt thanks to my wife Brenda for supporting my writing habit, especially on those bluebird days when we should have been out blazing trails together.

OTHER BOOKS BY JAMIE BASTEDO

FICTION

Tracking Triple Seven

On Thin Ice

Sila's Revenge (sequel to *On Thin Ice*)

Free as the Wind: Saving the Wild Horses of Sable Island

Nighthawk!

Cut Off

"Fever on Nipple Mountain," *The Horrors: Terrifying Tales, Book Two* (Peter Carver, editor)

NON-FICTION

Shield Country: Life and Times of the Oldest Piece of the Planet

Reaching North: A Celebration of the Subarctic

Falling for Snow: A Naturalist's Journey into the World of Winter

Trans Canada Trail: Official Guide to the Northwest Territories

Blue Lake and Rocky Shore: A Field Guide to Yellowknife's Natural Areas

Northern Wild: Best of Contemporary Canadian Nature Writing (David Boyd, editor)

*Selfie taken near the summit of Cuba's highest mountain,
Pico Turquino*

JAMIE BASTEDO is a biologist turned storyteller who connects readers of all ages with the magic and mystery of nature. His books for young readers include the novels, *Nighthawk!, On Thin Ice, Sila's Revenge, Tracking Triple Seven,* and the picture book, *Free As The Wind: Saving the Wild Horses of Sable Island.* His latest novel, *Cut Off,* about a cyberaddict "screenager" who finds deliverance on a wild northern river, earned a *Kirkus* Starred Review and Best Teen Fiction award. Formerly of Yellowknife, NWT, Jamie now lives in a lively cohousing community in the mountains near Nelson, BC.

PHOTO CREDITS